Compendium of
Cardmaking
Techniques

SEARCH PRESS

First published in Great Britain 2005

Search Press Limited
Wellwood, North Farm Road,
Tunbridge Wells, Kent TN2 3DR

Reprinted 2005

Based on the following books from the *Handmade Greetings Cards* series published by Search Press:

Tea Bag Folded Greetings Cards by Kim Reygate (2003)
Iris Folded Greetings Cards by Michelle Powell (2004)
Lacé Greetings Cards by Melanie Hendrick (2003)
Peel-Off Greetings Cards by Judy Balchin (2003)
Embroidered Greetings Cards by Dorothy Wood (2004)
Punched Greetings Cards by Julie Hickey (2003)
Silk Painted Greetings Cards by Mandy Southan (2003)
Glass Painted Greetings Cards by Judy Balchin (2002)
Metal & Wire Greetings Cards by Julie Hickey (2002)
Polymer Clay Greetings Cards by Candida Woolhouse (2002)
Rubber Stamped Greetings Cards by Melanie Hendrick (2002)
Embossed Greetings Cards by Carol Wallis (2004)

Text copyright © Judy Balchin, Melanie Hendrick, Julie Hickey , Michelle Powell, Kim Reygate, Mandy Southan , Carol Wallis, Dorothy Wood, Candida Woodhouse

Photographs by Charlotte de la Bédoyère, Search Press Studios and Roddy Paine Photographic Studios

Photographs and design copyright © Search Press Ltd. 2005

ISBN 1 84448 073 9

The Publishers and author can accept no responsibility for any consequences arising from the information, advice or instructions given in this publication.

Suppliers
If you have difficulty in obtaining any of the materials and equipment mentioned in this book, then please visit the Search Press website for details of suppliers:
www.searchpress.com

Alternatively, you can write to the Publishers at the address above, for a current list of stockists, including firms who operate a mail-order service.

Manufactured by Classicscan Pte Ltd, Singapore

Printed in Malaysia by Times Offset (M) Sdn Bhd

Contents

Introduction

Imagine the delight of your friend or loved one when they open an envelope with your handwriting on the front and discover a handmade card inside. They will be touched that you have taken the time and trouble to make something unique just for them. Making a card is as much a pleasure as receiving one and you have a huge selection of innovative and attractive designs to choose from in this book. Even if you have never considered yourself artistic before, you can make a card that someone else will treasure. You do not need years of craft experience as each project is clearly explained and accompanied by simple step-by-step photography.

Nine professional artists have been brought together here to share their ideas and expertise. Though their styles are diverse they all have a talent for explaining their craft clearly and inspiring creativity in others. So whether you are a beginner or an accomplished crafter wishing to expand your repertoire, there is an exciting range of different crafts to explore in this compendium.

There is a clear description of the basic materials required for all the crafts at the beginning of the book, followed by a guide to making a blank card to get you started. At the start of each project you will find a list of the specific equipment, including quantities and dimensions, needed for that particular card.

So gather together your arty bits and pieces, clear a table and set aside some time to create your own mini masterpiece.

Materials

Paper

You will need a selection of papers and there is a vast range available in all colours, thicknesses and finishes. In addition to plain coloured paper, experiment with handmade, pearlescent, foil, patterned and shimmer paper for background panels. Vellum and parchment paper are just two of the names used for translucent paper. You can embroider on to translucent paper or layer it to create a distinctive background panel. Thin papers are best for iris folding and tea bag folding requires tea bag squares which can be bought in printed sheets.

Card

The basic ingredient of any card-making project is the card stock itself. You can buy ready-made card blanks or make your own. A huge variety of card is available, in many colours and shapes, some with a metallic, holographic or pearlescent finish, some printed with a background design, or a different colour on each side such as duo card. When choosing card for card making, remember that it must be able to support your artwork and decorative panels can get quite heavy, so a thicker card is better.

Basic materials

There is some basic craft equipment that will be useful for all the projects in this book. Firstly, graphite **pencils** in various weights from HB to the softer grades (B to 8B). To create cards and mounts you will need a **ruler** and a **set square** for measuring, and a **cutting mat**, a **craft knife** and a **metal ruler** for cutting. Alternatively you could invest in a **rotary trimmer** or **craft guillotine** to cut your cards and papers. **Tracing paper** is invaluable for transferring designs. A **bone folder** will help you to score and fold card effectively. There are a number of adhesive tapes that you will find useful including: **double-sided sticky tape**, **masking tape** and **low tack tape**.

A selection of basic equipment used in card making.

Similarly, there are various glues that will prove indispensible such as **all-purpose glue**, **spray adhesive**, **fast-acting paper glue**, **glue stick** and **adhesive putty**. **Tweezers** are useful for handling delicate or small parts of your work. **3D foam squares** raise up sections of your design to give a three-dimensional effect. **Pins** and **split pins** are useful additions to your workbox. Using **eyelets** is a neat method of fixing paper to card. You will also need an **eyelet setting tool, piercing tool** and **hammer**.

Embellishments

Build up a collection of attractive bits and pieces so that you can dip into it whenever you are making cards. **Flat-backed gem stones** add sparkle and unusual **buttons, beads, charms, ribbons** and **sequins** can all be attached to your cards to give them a new dimension. **3D paint** and **gel pens** can be used for accents such as dots. **Glitter spray** creates shimmer. A pair of **crimpers** or **fancy-edged scissors** will give your backgrounds and cards decorative edges. **Peel-offs** are craft stickers that can be used as embellishments or as the central focus of the card. **Wire** has a variety of decorative uses and can be shaped with **round-nosed pliers**.

Other materials

Some of the projects in this book are based on specific crafts and require a small number of specialist materials.

Punches

Punches come in many different shapes, sizes and designs. They range from single hole plier punches to small, medium, large and even super giant punches, long reach punches, thumbnail punches and border punches.

Lacé

Lacé is essentially a cutting system and kits are available that contain everything you will need. A Lacé kit comprises: templates, cutting mat, knife and spare blades, score and fold tool, ruler and low-tack tape.

Embroidery

A lightweight plain weave fabric such as **Panama fabric** is ideal for embroidery. Add a top layer of **silk organza** to give a subtle touch of colour. **Fine cotton lawn or poplin** is an ideal backing fabric. Place your layers of fabric in an **embroidery hoop** while you stitch using **six-stranded embroidery cotton**. For best results, separate all six strands of the cotton first and then thread the required number in the needle. For stitching on **felt** use **coton perlé** or **three-ply pima cotton**.

Silk painting

Habotai No. 8 is an inexpensive, multi-purpose silk that is ideal for cards. Using a **wooden frame** prevents the silk touching the work surface when outlining or painting, so the colours can spread evenly and are contained by the resist lines. **Resist** or **outliner** blocks the silk fibres, preventing colours spreading to adjoining areas. **Iron-fix paints** are ironed to bond the colours to the silk. (Use a cotton cloth to protect your ironing board and a hot, dry iron on the reverse of the silk so it does not stick to the outliner.) You only need a few basic colours: two reds, two yellows and two blues. From these you can mix greens, oranges and violets and a wide range of neutral tones. **Droppers** are useful for transferring colours or adding water to dilute them.

A craft heating tool can be used for melting embossing powders and setting pigment ink. It will also heat copper (see page 150). Take care as the nozzle gets very hot. Use the tool on a heatproof surface.

Rubber stamping

There is an enormous variety of commercially made **rubber stamps** available. Slow-drying pigment inks are applied directly to the stamp. **Pigment inks** can also be used to bind **embossing powders**, tiny granules of powder that melt to a raised glossy finish when heat is applied.

Polymer clay

There are various brands of **polymer clay** available, each with slightly different handling characteristics. Keep opened blocks of clay in **resealable plastic bags** in a cool dark place. Model the clay on a **white ceramic tile** and then bake, on the tile, in a domestic oven, following the instructions on the packet. Take care to monitor the temperature, as burning clay can give off toxic fumes. Use **metal or wooden tools** as the plasticiser in the unbaked clay can affect plastic ones. Use greenware clay work tools, ball-ended and pointed embossing tools and an extra firm clay shaper with a rubbery tip which smoothes out blemishes.

Glass painting

Glass paints are transparent and ideal for painting on **acetate**. **Water-based glass paints** dry quickly and have very little odour. Do not use water to dilute them as this will affect the viscosity – use clear paint from the same range. **Brushes** used with water-based paints can be cleaned with water.

Metal and wire

Metal is available in copper, brass, pewter and aluminium and comes in both light and medium weights. Copper metal changes from its bright copper colour to tarnished orange, then to pink, purple and blue and finally to silvery gold when heated. **Coloured foils** are much thinner and lighter weight than the metals. You cannot change the colour of the foils by heating them. **Wire** is available in many gauges and colours, and is easy to shape. The higher the gauge number, the thinner the wire, e.g. 26g is thinner than 18g. Wire is sold by length and by weight, in pounds or kilos. **Wire cutters** are best for cutting wire, since if you use scissors, you will damage them.

Making cards

Card blanks are widely available but making your own cards will give you the freedom to select exactly the colour, card, size and aperture shape that you want. The card on to which you mount your artwork is as important as the artwork itself. Avoid cheap card – if you have spent your precious creative time making a piece of artwork, it deserves to be mounted on the best quality card you can afford.

The card has to be of a weight that can support your artwork. The copper metal can make it quite heavy, so a thin card would buckle and bend. The weights of card vary from colour to colour and between different textures too. This means that there is no magic number to work from, but around 160gsm is a good average weight card, and dark coloured card will probably need to be more like 240gsm.

Once you have chosen a card in the colour you want, of a weight to support your artwork, test it to feel how firm it is, making sure that it will not bend too much.

Scoring and folding

1. Cut your card to size using a paper trimmer, or a metal ruler and a craft knife, on a self-healing cutting mat.

2. Measure your card to find the centre, and put a small pencil mark at the top and bottom.

3. Remove the blade from the paper trimmer and place the card under the trimmer guide. Place a bone folder in an upright position in the cutting groove and pull it down to the bottom of the card several times. Apply only light pressure.

4. Remove the card and you will see a groove called 'the valley'. This is the front of your card. Rub off the pencil marks with a plastic eraser.

5. Turn the card over and you will see a bulbous line. This is 'the mountain,' and this is always on the inside of the card. Put the edges of the card together and use the bone folder on its side to flatten the fold of the card. This will give it a sharp, crisp edge.

Mounting

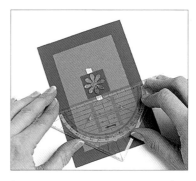

1. To mount card to card, apply double-sided tape to all the edges of the card to be mounted. Pull the paper backing off just a little. Working from the front, you can see little tabs showing.

2. Place this card on your folded card. Since only parts of the double-sided tape are exposed, you can move it around to position it. When you are happy with the position, firm the exposed corners down. Hold the card in place and gently pull the tabs of backing paper away. Now firm along all the edges.

3. Use a set square to mark the position of your finished artwork. This set square has ruler markings that work from the nought in the centre outwards in both directions. This makes it easy to place your artwork in the centre of your card.

Tea Bag Folding

by Kim Reygate

So what is tea bag folding, I hear you ask. It has little to do with soggy wet tea bags, it is simple origami using small decorative squares of paper. The origins of this papercraft lie in the Netherlands where tea bags were enclosed in pretty paper envelopes which were then used as the basis for creating beautiful rosettes – hence 'tea bag' folding. Tea bag papers, papers printed with small square designs, are now available specifically for this papercraft.

I started teaching tea bag folding in 1998 and I soon became known as the 'Bag Lady' because I always arrived at my classes laden with lots of bags. I have since played with, and taught, just about everything to do with stamping and papercraft but my regular students still think of me as the Bag Lady from those first tea bag folding classes.

I hope that the following pages will inspire you to begin tea bag folding. Just about any type of paper can be used to create a square, which can then be folded and transformed into wonderful rosettes. You will discover how to make three types of folds; square, triangle and kite. I then show how to incorporate a square-folded rosette into a beautiful card. Complete the project and then experiment on your own with the folds I have given you.

I do not throw anything away because there will always come a time when I might need that little scrap of 'waste'. As I strive to use up all those little left-over pieces, I am constantly reminded of something said by one of my mentors – 'It's never a mistake, it's always an opportunity'.

I hope that these words inspire you in the same way.

Kim x

Basic folds

Just three basic folds are used to make all the projects in this book: the square, the triangle and the kite. Master these folds and you can create a kaleidoscope of different designs. A single design of printed tea bag square can produce four different patterns from each type of fold. When the folds are assembled, each pattern will produce two different rosettes; one by placing the folds left over right, the other by placing them right over left. When you have mastered a fold with tea bag squares, try folding squares cut from other types of paper – a random design in each square creates a stunning finish.

You will need
Sheet of printed tea
bag papers
Scissors or
craft knife and
cutting mat

Square fold

This is probably the easiest fold to start with and it will lead you on a journey of discovery. You will need eight identical tea bag squares.

1. Start by folding a paper, side to side.

2. Use a bone folder to crease the fold.

3. Open the paper, then fold and crease the other sides.

4. Open the paper, turn it over, fold corner to corner, then crease the diagonal.

5. Open the paper, then fold and crease the other diagonal.

6. Open the paper and check the folds.

7. Turn the paper over, then using the creases as a guide, start to close the fold.

8. Flatten the paper to form a small square. Repeat steps 1–7 with the other seven papers, ensuring that each square has the same design at the front.

9. Apply a dab of all-purpose adhesive.

10. Insert another paper snugly inside the first so that the bottom points are aligned. Here I am assembling the folds left over right.

11. Close the fold, and press the glued pieces together.

12. Repeat steps 10–11 with the other six papers to complete the rosette.

One design of tea bag square can create four different square folds, each of which can be assembled to produce two different finished rosettes.

The open sides of the square folds in the left-hand column were trimmed with deckle-edged scissors before being assembled (see page 18).

Triangle fold

This fold is made by reversing the steps used for the square fold on pages 16–17. It is probably the most versatile of the three folds in that, with a little modification, it can also be used to create non-rosette shapes. You will need eight identical tea bag squares and deckle-edged scissors to trim the open edge of each triangle fold.

1. Fold a paper corner to corner. Use the bone folder to crease the diagonal (see page 16).

2. Open the paper, then fold the other corners together and crease the diagonal.

3. Open the paper, turn it over, then fold it side to side.

4. Fold and crease the other sides, then open the paper and check the folds.

5. Close the folds to form a triangle, ensuring that your chosen image appears on the front face. Repeat steps 1–5 with the other seven papers.

6. Use deckle-edged scissors to trim the open edges of the fold. This neatens any uneven folding.

7. Referring to page 17, apply a dab of adhesive to one fold, then insert a second fold snugly inside the first. Ensure that the bottom points of the folds are aligned.

8. Close the fold, and press the glued pieces together. This example shows a left over right assembly.

9. Repeat steps 6–8 with the other six papers to complete the rosette.

One design of tea bag square can create four different triangle folds, each of which can be assembled to produce two different finished rosettes.

The open edges at the top of the folds used in the right-hand column were trimmed with deckle-edged scissors before being assembled (see page 18).

Kite (or nappy) fold

This fold is slightly more complex than the square and triangle folds, not in the folding, but in the assembly of the rosette. You will need eight identical tea bag squares. The folds must be assembled at the correct angles (see step 8) so that they form a tight circle. Any deviation will make it almost impossible to perform the final manoeuvre, and a lopsided or buckled rosette will result.

When using printed tea bag squares it is essential to decide which of the four corners is to form the points of the rosette; the first fold must be made through this corner.

1. Fold a paper corner to corner through your chosen top point.

2. Open the paper, take one of the sides across to the fold line, then carefully crease along this diagonal.

3. Repeat with the opposite side to form this shape.

4. Fold the bottom point up as shown.

5. Open the fold, turn the paper over, then fold up the bottom point along the crease made in step 4. Repeat steps 1–5 with the other seven papers, ensuring that same design appears on each fold.

6. Turn the paper over and apply a small dab of adhesive to the right-hand corner of the fold as shown.

7. Turn the paper over again and insert the glued corner in the top of the centre opening of a second kite fold . . .

8. . . . then carefully slide the paper down until it is positioned as shown. Working clockwise, repeat steps 6–8 to assemble the other six kite folds.

Tip

In this demonstration the kite folds were assembled right into left. To assemble folds left into right, apply adhesive to the left-hand corner in step 6.

9. To attach the last fold to the first, turn the rosette over and dab adhesive on to the exposed corner of the last fold . . .

10. . . . turn the rosette over again and carefully bring the last fold to the front . . .

11. . . . then slide the glued corner of the last fold into the opening of the first.

One design of tea bag square can create four different kite folds. Each variation of fold can be assembled left into right or right into left (see steps 6 and 7) to produce two different finished rosettes.

The two top sides of the folds used for the rosettes in the right-hand column were trimmed with deckle-edged scissors before being assembled.

Eastern Promise

Inspiration for a card design can come from all sorts of places – as soon as I saw these serviettes I knew exactly what I wanted to create with them. Serviettes can make great backgrounds, but once you have attached them to paper (using a spray adhesive) there should be nothing to stop you tea bag folding with them. Serviettes are usually two or three ply, and you must always separate the top, printed layer from the others before sticking it to paper to prevent it coming adrift once it has been stuck down.

You will need

Single-fold black square card
Gold and white paper
Serviette
Rubber stamp cube
Brass detail embossing powder, embossing ink pad and heat tool
Clean-up pad and paper towel
Scissors
Rotary trimmer or craft knife, metal ruler and cutting mat
Bone folder
Spray adhesive
Double-sided sticky tape (DSST)

1. Carefully strip away the top, printed layer of the serviette.

2. Using an old cardboard box as a spray booth, apply spray adhesive to the sheet of white paper . . .

3. . . . then place the printed layer of the serviette on to the adhesive and smooth it down with your hands.

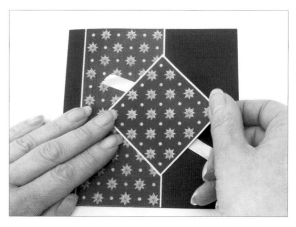

4. Cut a 6cm x 13cm (2¼ x 5in) rectangle and a 6cm (2¼in) square from the mounted serviette, then use strips of DSST to attach these to the gold paper.

5. Trim the gold paper to leave a narrow border round the square and down the long edges of the rectangle. Use strips of DSST to attach the rectangle and then the square on the single-fold black card.

6. Dab clear embossing ink on the stamp . . .

7. . . . then stamp an image on to the sheet of gold paper.

8. Sprinkle brass detail embossing powder over the stamped image . . .

9. . . . tap off the excess powder . . .

10. . . . then use the heat tool to emboss the image. Leave to cool.

11. Repeat steps 6–10 to make a further seven images, leaving a gap between each. Cut the stamped images into squares.

12. Referring to pages 16–17 make eight square folds, then, using small pieces of DSST (rather than adhesive), assemble the folded papers into a rosette.

13. Use two strips of DSST to attach the rosette to the card.

Tips for cleaning rubber stamps

Baby wipes are ideal for cleaning rubber stamps, but must be alcohol-free.

A damp stamp-cleaning mat can also be used.

If you ever apply waterproof or archival inks to rubber stamps, a solvent-based cleaner must be used.

NEVER clean your rubber stamps under the tap!

14. Fold and trim a gold insert to size, then use strips of DSST to attach it to the card.

The finished card with matching gift tag and envelope.

Oriental Flower

This card is a combination of rubber stamped and embossed images, torn strips of handmade, patterned paper and a square-fold rosette made from printed tea bag papers.

Golden Vellum

The rosette on this card which was created from the decorated vellum, is a variation of the normal square-fold rosette. Here, I used scallop-edged punches to cut four large squares and four small ones. The rosette was assembled using alternate large and small squares.

Golden Orient

The rosette used on this card was made from a slightly thicker paper than normal, on which the design had been rubber-stamped and embossed. The thick paper led to a larger hole being left in the centre of the rosette, so I glued on a button to hide the hole. Having made the rosette, I searched for a suitable card on which to mount it. I came across the perfect answer in a three-fold aperture card with a gold circle that matched the size of the rosette. I did not need the three folds so I stuck the top two layers together with strips of DSST.

Eastern Delight

This is a variation of the serviette card (see page 25). I always try to customise the envelope for the finished card by using some of the left-over materials to embellish its edge.

Iris Folding

by Michelle Powell

The first time I saw an iris folded card, I was mesmerised by the swirling, spiralling layers of paper. The rich, intricate design looked very complicated, with layers of interest in every fold of the beautiful handmade paper. When I set about trying to make the folded panel, I was amazed at how simple it was to create such a complex-looking design, just by following a basic pattern.

The overlapping, spiralling layers of folded paper that create an iris folded design look similar to the iris aperture in a camera lens, which is how iris folding got its name. Like many paper crafts, iris folding originated in the Netherlands. The inside of Dutch envelopes are often printed with a pretty pattern, and strips of this paper were used to create iris folded designs.

A simple folded design enhances the beauty of the papers used, letting them speak for themselves rather than consigning them to a border or a background. I am a self-confessed paper junky: I love browsing through books of printed paper or touching sheets of vellum, pearlescent paper or glittery card. You do not need to spend a fortune, though; iris folding can be done with wrapping paper or whatever type of paper appeals to you, as long as it is not too thick.

The following projects will guide you through the basic technique of iris folding, explaining how to cut, fold, and most importantly, position all those wonderful papers. When you have mastered the basic technique, let your imagination run wild and try creating your own designs.

Basic techniques

Some basic crafting skills will help you complete the iris folding projects included in this compendium. There are many ways to complete these basic techniques, but I have shown you the way I find easiest.

You will need
Ruler
Pencil
Card
Cutting mat
Craft knife
Embossing sylus or bone folder
Tracing paper
Double-sided tape
Scissors
Coloured papers
White paper

Folding and scoring card

1. Use a ruler and pencil to measure and mark your card to the size and shape that you need.

2. Put your work on a cutting mat and use a craft knife and ruler to cut out the card.

3. Mark the centre point at the top and bottom of the card using a pencil.

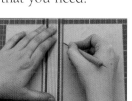

4. Place a ruler on your card to join these marks and use an embossing stylus or bone folder to score the card.

5. Fold the card, making sure that the top edges line up. Trim the card if the edges are out of line. Use your thumbnail to reinforce the fold.

Transferring patterns

To transfer patterns, I prefer to create a set of card templates. It takes a little longer, but your templates can be used many times over.

1. Trace the pattern directly from the book using tracing paper and a pencil.

2. Cover a piece of thin card with double-sided tape and stick the tracing paper pattern to it.

3. Cut round the pattern using scissors or a craft knife and cutting mat.

4. Draw around the template on to the correct coloured paper or card.

Cutting and folding paper strips

Cut strips of paper are used for most of the projects in this book, they are quick and simple to make. When using very translucent vellum, cut the strips, but do not fold.

1. Use a ruler and pencil to measure strips 1.5cm (⅝in) wide (some projects will require wider strips).

2. Use a craft knife, cutting mat and ruler to cut the strips. It does not matter if they are a bit wobbly as you use the folded rather than the cut edge.

3. Fold approximately one third of the paper over. Most papers can be folded by hand, but for stiff papers, place a ruler on the strip, score along it using an embossing stylus, then fold.

Making a key

A key is useful to help you remember which coloured strip goes where when you are making up the iris folded panel.

1. Mark up a piece of card with six rows and two columns. The size does not matter, as this is for your reference only.

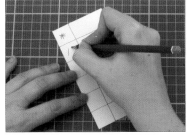

2. Draw each of the symbols used in this book in the left column. They are *, #, $, +, &, %. If you plan to do a lot of iris folding it may be worth laminating this key.

3. Attach a small square of each of your chosen coloured paper strips next to the correct symbol using adhesive putty. If your iris panel has four colours, use the top four; if it has five or six, use the top five or all six rows. After completing your iris design, remove the strips so that you can use the key again.

Simple Iris Folding

Iris folding creates such an intriguing pattern of swirling papers that sometimes a simple card is best to show off the beauty of the papers and the technique itself. For this first project you will need four attractive papers: combine patterned papers with different textures and finishes to get the most interesting results. These cards are suitable for all occasions and make great cards for men.

You will need

Turquoise card 21 x 15cm
(8¼ x 6in)

Cream card 8 x 8cm
(3¹/₈ x 3¹/₈in)

Orange shimmer paper

Orange patterned paper

Turquoise pearl paper

Turquoise patterned paper

Orange patterned card

5 orange eyelets

Craft knife and cutting mat

Scissors

Ruler and pencil

Glue stick or glue roller

Double-sided tape

Eyelet setting tool and hammer

Hole punch

Adhesive putty

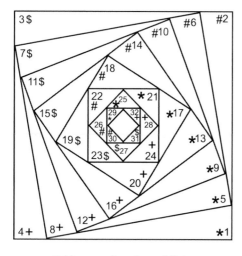

Folding template shown full size

KEY:

* Turquoise patterned

Orange shimmer

$ Turquoise pearl

+ Orange patterned

1. Cut a square of cream card 8 x 8cm (3¹/₈ x 3¹/₈in). Measure and mark a 7 x 7cm (2¾ x 2¾in) aperture in the centre of this card, leaving a 1cm (½in) border on all sides. This will be trimmed to a narrower border later.

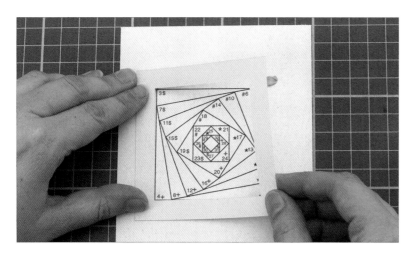

2. You can use the folding template directly from the page, but if you don't want to get glue on your book, photocopy or trace it first. Use small pieces of adhesive putty to hold the aperture card in place on top of the template. You will build up the design from the back.

3. Cut and fold the paper strips as shown on page 31. For this project you will need approximately 40cm (15¾in) in length for each of the four colours, but this does not have to be one long length.

Tip
To save time you can cut all four strips for one loop to length in one go, since the strips for each side are the same length.

4. Make a key (see page 31). Start with segment 1 on the outer edge and place a strip of your first coloured paper marked *. Place it face down, lining up the folded edge with the diagonal line. Use a pencil to mark where you need to trim the paper.

5. Cut the paper strip to length. Apply a line of glue around the aperture where you are about to place the strip. Do not put any glue on the template.

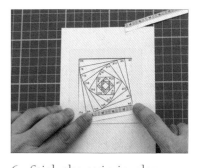

6. Stick the strip in place, being careful to line up the folded edge with the diagonal line.

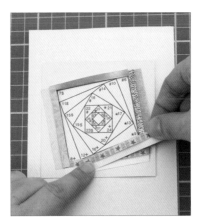

7. Move on to your second colour (marked with #), line up and cut the strip as before. Glue it into position on the right-hand side of the aperture in the outer segment marked with a 2.

8. Repeat with your third colour marked $ and fourth marked + so that you have one piece on each of the four sides of the square aperture. Start again with your first colour marked *. Measure, mark and cut the strip, lining it up with the second diagonal line on segment 5. Place the glue on the back of the first strip when you glue the next strip into position.

9. Continue measuring, marking, cutting and gluing strips following the numbers and changing colour to match each symbol.

10. Continue, creating one full loop each time until you reach the middle. Cut a small piece of paper and glue it over the central hole.

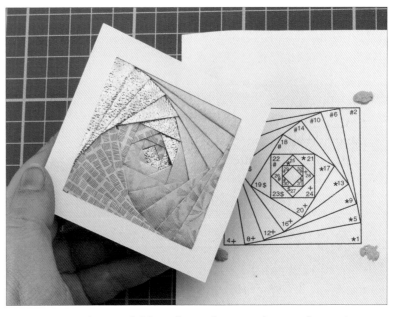

11. Remove the iris folding from the template and turn it over to reveal the design.

12. Cover the back of the iris folding with double-sided tape; this will help to hold all the pieces in position.

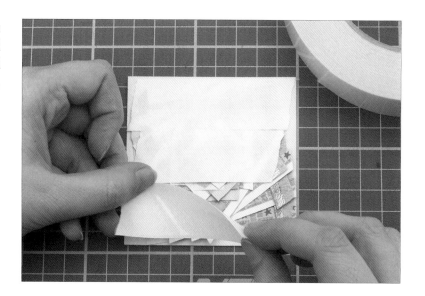

13. Trim the aperture border to 0.5cm (¼in), cutting through the aperture, the edges of the folded strips and the double-sided tape all at once.

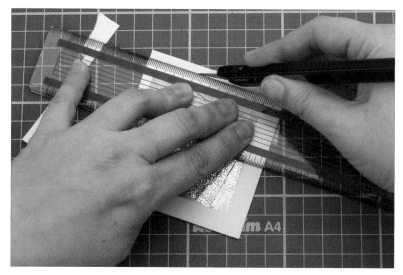

14. Use an A6 folded turquoise card blank or cut and fold your own. Cut a strip of orange patterned paper 3.5 x 15cm (1½ x 6in). Place this on the right-hand edge of the card, then place the iris folded piece on top. Position five eyelets on the orange strip and mark their centres using a pencil.

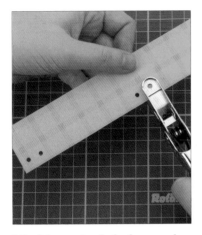

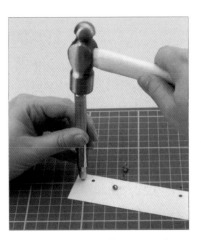

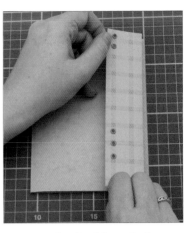

15. Use a single hole punch with a hole the same size as your eyelets to make five holes over the pencil marks on the orange patterned strip.

16. Place an eyelet in each hole, turn the strip over and use the setting tool and hammer to curl down the back of each eyelet.

17. Apply double-sided tape to the back of the orange strip and stick it in place on the turquoise card.

18. Remove the backing from the double-sided tape on the back of the iris folding and stick it in place on the card to finish.

The finished card is reminiscent of the sea with its suggestion of swirling blue waves and golden shimmering sands.

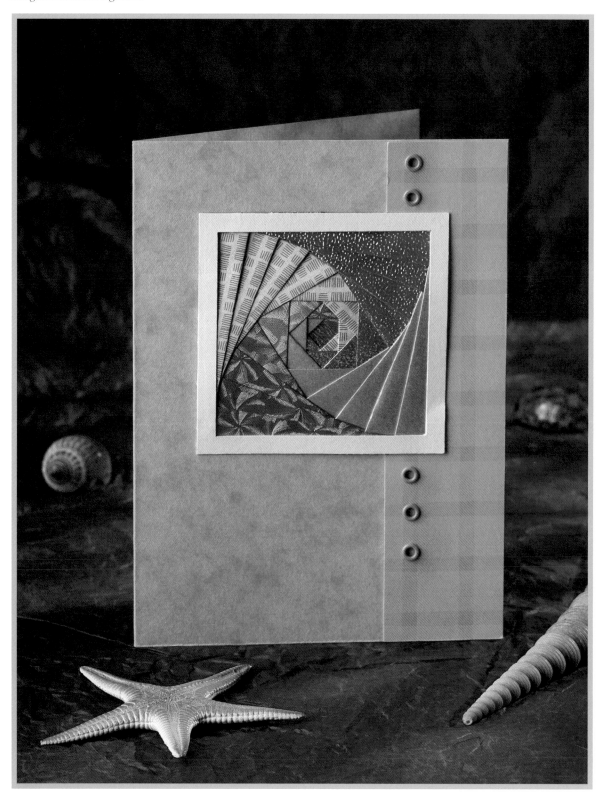

Use these folding templates straight from the page or enlarge them on a photocopier to the size you require. The templates were enlarged to 125% to make the cards shown opposite.

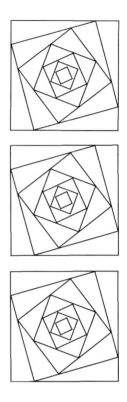

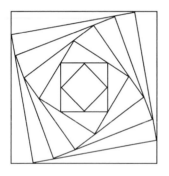

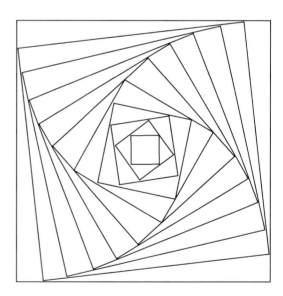

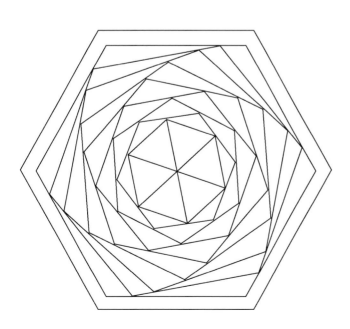

Use a variety of coloured and textured papers to make your simple iris folded cards look stunning.

Photo Folding

You can achieve an iris folded effect with photographs even though the technique you use is very different. It would be impossible to cut strips of photographs that would then line up perfectly to recreate the image. Instead you use multiple copies of the same image; each one becomes one layer of folding. Most copy shops will photocopy a photograph for you, or if you have a home printer you can print out multiple copies of the same image. Photocopy your initial image if you do not want to cut the original photograph.

You will need

5 identical photographic images

Yellow card 15 x 29.7cm (5⅞ x 11¾in)

Green pearlescent paper, 11 x 14cm (4⅜ x 5½in)

White card 11cm x 11cm (4⅜ x 4⅜in)

Lemon check paper 15cm x 6.5cm (6 x 2½in)

A4 photocopy acetate or tracing paper

Scrap of white paper

Small daisy and leaf punches

3 orange flat-backed gemstones

Craft knife and cutting mat

Embossing stylus

Ruler and pencil

Double-sided tape in various widths

All-purpose glue

Adhesive putty

Pin

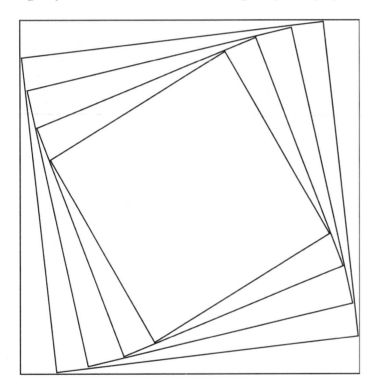

Folding template shown full size

Tip

Choose either a simple close-up photograph and create the iris folding over the image, or choose a photograph with a large background area and create an iris folded surround from the background.

1. Photocopy the folding template on to acetate or trace it on to tracing paper. Place this on the photograph and move it around to decide which part of the picture you want to focus on.

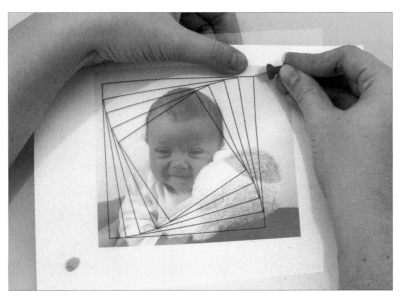

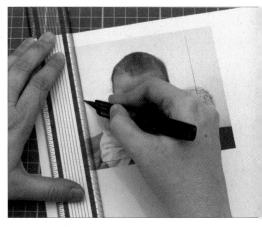

2. Fix the acetate iris folding template in position on the photograph with adhesive putty. Use a pin to mark a hole through the acetate and photograph in each corner of the outside edge of the template.

3. Join the pin dots to cut out the square of the picture that you need using a craft knife and cutting mat. Colour photocopy or print out this image five times, spacing the images to leave a plain border around each image.

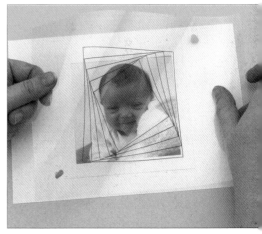

4. Take your square of white card and cut an aperture hole 9 x 9cm (3½ x 3½ in) in the centre using a craft knife and cutting mat. Place double-sided tape around the edges of the aperture and stick it to one of the photos, lining up its inside edges with the outside edge of the photograph.

5. Place the acetate copy of the folding template back on the image with the aperture attached and hold it in place using adhesive putty. Make a pin hole in each corner of the next square in on the folding template.

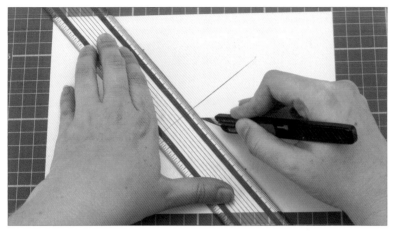

6. Remove the template, turn the image over and cut diagonally from pin hole to pin hole. Repeat with the remaining two pin holes to make a large cut cross.

7. Use an embossing stylus to score a square shape, joining the pin holes on the back of the image.

8. Fold the image on each of the score lines so that the centre of the image is folded over to the back.

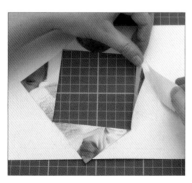

9. Use strips of double-sided tape to hold the cut flaps flat to the back of the image.

10. Add more double-sided tape around the edge of the hole, ready to assemble the iris design later.

11. Take another of the photographic images and attach the acetate folding template to it using adhesive putty. Use a pin to mark the corners of the next square in on the template.

12. Repeat steps 6 to 11 above to cut, score, fold and attach tape to this image with a slightly smaller square hole in the centre.

13. Repeat steps 5 to 11 with the next two photographic images, each time moving in one square. Leave the last image intact.

14. To assemble the iris folding, start with the intact photographic image and stick the image with the smallest hole in place first. Take care to line up the images correctly.

15. Build up the picture a layer at a time, using the image with the largest hole and the aperture frame last.

16. Cut a square of green pearlescent paper 11 x 11cm (4³/₈ x 4³/₈in). Stick the iris folded image to the middle of this piece using double-sided tape.

17. Take your piece of yellow card. Score it in the middle and fold it in half. Take your rectangle of lemon check paper, apply double-sided tape to the back and stick it in place along the bottom of the yellow folded card.

18. Punch three small daisies from white paper, and four small leaves from green pearlescent paper.

19. Glue a flat-backed gemstone to the middle of each flower using all-purpose glue.

20. Use all-purpose glue to attach the daisies and leaves to the bottom of the card. Use double-sided tape to attach the iris folding and border to the middle of the card.

The finished card would make a wonderful birth announcement card or a keepsake for the baby's first birthday.

45

Use these folding templates straight from the page or enlarge them on a photocopier to the size you require. The templates were enlarged to 118% to make the cards shown opposite.

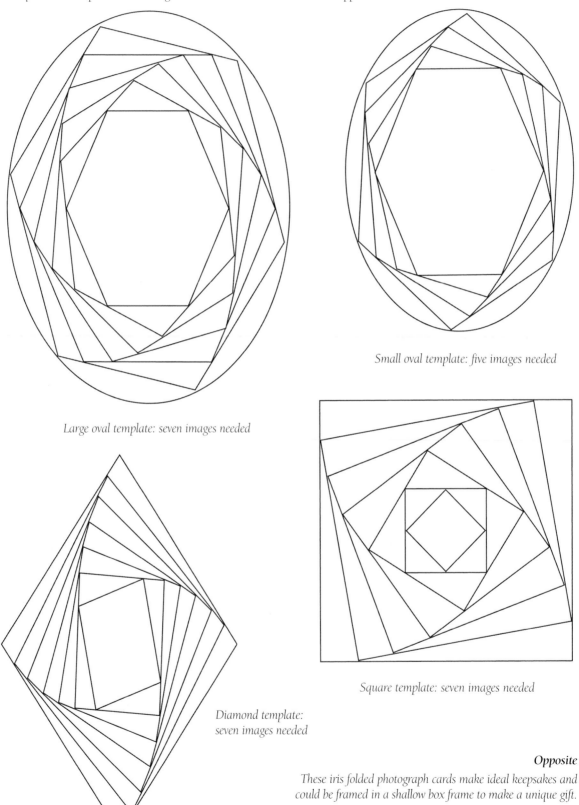

Small oval template: five images needed

Large oval template: seven images needed

Square template: seven images needed

Diamond template:
seven images needed

Opposite
These iris folded photograph cards make ideal keepsakes and could be framed in a shallow box frame to make a unique gift.

Lacé

by Melanie Hendrick

As a creative person I am always on the lookout for something new to keep my cards fresh and innovative. So you can imagine my excitement when a friend from Holland sent me a couple of bright green templates with matching tools, a technique book in Dutch and a note to encourage me to have a go at Lacé, which was becoming a popular craft technique in Europe.

I quickly became hooked. The Lacé technique began to dominate my card making, mixing perfectly with my addiction to rubber stamping (see page 168) and other papercrafts.

The term Lacé comes from a French word meaning 'linked together'. It began as a selection of products, but because of its popularity it has evolved into a technique of its own. Lacé involves cutting the template designs from two-toned paper, card or vellum. When you fold the cut flaps over, they reveal the contrasting colour. You then tuck each flap under the piece in front to create that 'linked together' effect.

No matter how you use the Lacé technique, you are guaranteed to create stunning cards that will delight the recipient and bring you hours of fun and delight in the creation.

Get ready to embark on a new creative adventure. Happy creating!

Melanie x

Basic techniques

The Lacé technique is not for quick card making. Time must be taken, combined with a little know-how, to achieve the beautiful Lacé effect. 'Practise' and 'relax' are words I recall from when I first started working with the Lacé knife. Since the blade is cut at a 45° angle, it is important to hold it at that angle when applying pressure, so that you cut cleanly through your card. If you can get the cutting right, the rest of the steps flow easily.

You will need

Lacé template 3
Lacé knife and spare blades
Lacé score and fold tool
Lacé ruler
Lacé cutting mat
Low tack tape
Card blanks
Permanent marker

1. Open your card blank and place it on your Lacé cutting mat. Position the template on the open card. Centre the template on the front and secure it with low tack tape. Mark the template with a reference point, so that you will know where you started cutting.

2. Put the Lacé knife in at a 90° angle. Punch the tip of the blade through the card to the cutting mat.

3. Relax the position in which you are holding the knife, until you are holding it as you would a pen.

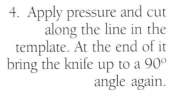

4. Apply pressure and cut along the line in the template. At the end of it bring the knife up to a 90° angle again.

5. Rotate the cutting mat and start the other side of the cut, holding the knife at a 90° angle again. Go round the template cutting all the V shapes in the same way, ending at your reference mark, where you started.

6. Remove the template to reveal your cut design.

7. Position the Lacé ruler at the base of one of your cut shapes, so that it joins up the base cuts, and use the Lacé score and fold tool to score a line.

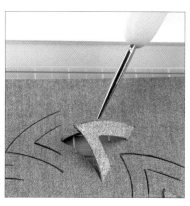

8. Lift up the flap with the same tool.

9. Flip the score and fold tool over and fold the flap with the other end.

10. Fold all the flaps up in the same way.

11. Tuck each folded back flap under the flap behind it.

The finished card

Using templates 2–21

Templates 2–21 have been made to be used as you see them. Simply follow the cutting lines. What makes these templates fun to work with is that they are available in a wonderful assortment of designs, producing very individual results.

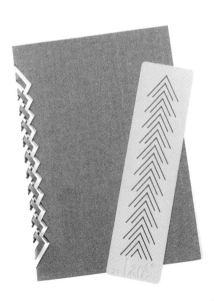

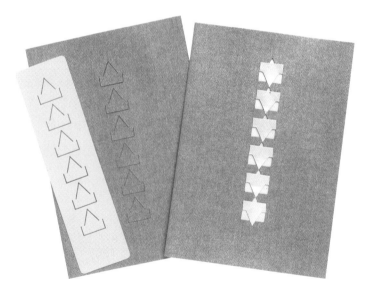

This bookmark template 21 has been used to decorate the spine of a card.

Template 12 is a flip and fold bookmark template, shown here with a cut card and a second card showing the flipped and folded effect.

Template 5 with the cut and folded results

Template 6 with a cut card, and a second card showing the camera aperture effect produced by folding

Using templates 22–34

Templates 22–34 have been designed so that you can be really creative with them. Use them as you see them, or try skipping some of the cutting lines to create thicker folds, or a combination of thick and thin folds. With one template you can create multiple results.

All these results were produced using template 27. On the left is a card showing the cutting lines before folding – you can see that some of the cutting lines have been skipped. How many variations can you come up with?

Memory Lane Tag Book

I am an avid traveller, and photographs are my way of capturing special moments, crazy adventures and spectacular sites. They also allow me to take with me precious visual reminders of those I am parted from, however briefly.

This project is a mixture of basic book-making techniques, collage and creative machine stitching, allowing you to surround your photographs with delicate Lacé frames and preserve them in a beautiful tag book. I am sure that as you read this, a photograph has sprung to mind that deserves this special treatment. Go and dig it out and join me on a wonderful creative journey.

You will need

Lacé templates 33 and 12, knife and blades, score and fold tool, ruler and cutting mat

Low tack tape

Two aqua and two turquoise duo card tags, 203 x 64mm (8 x 2½in)

Two aqua and two turquoise duo card luggage labels, 82 x 38mm (3¼ x 1½in)

Scrap aqua and turquoise duo card

A4 lozenge printed vellum

Sewing machine

Paper scissors

18 gauge wire, wire cutters and round-nosed pliers

Plastic tube

Velvet ribbon in two shades

Double-sided tape

Circle and flower craft punches

Embroidery thread and heart-shaped button

3D foam squares

Landscape-shaped photograph

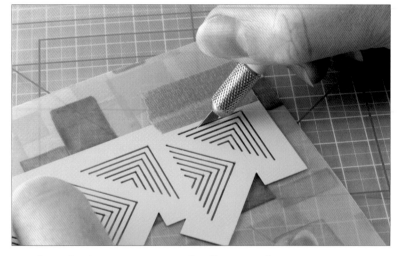

1. Place the lozenge-patterned vellum on the cutting mat, tape down template 33 and cut.

2. Fold back the cut shapes. Trim round the Lacé area leaving a 12mm (½in) border. Repeat to make a total of four vellum panels. Set aside.

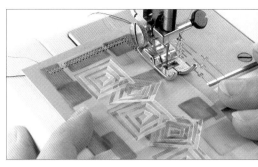

3. Cut two 61cm (24in) lengths of velvet ribbon in different shades. Stick a piece of double-sided tape on an aqua tag, 7.6cm (3in) from the top. Place a second piece 5cm (2in) lower down. Stick the ribbons on velvet-side down, 18cm (7in) from the end of each ribbon. Attach a turquoise tag further along the ribbon to the left, leaving a 1½cm (½in) gap between tags, and repeat with the other aqua and turquoise tags (see the diagram below).

4. Place the vellum panel centrally on a turquoise tag, over the ribbons, and stitch it in place using a sewing machine and turquoise thread. Repeat for the other three panels.

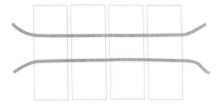

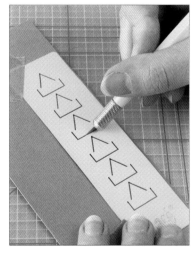

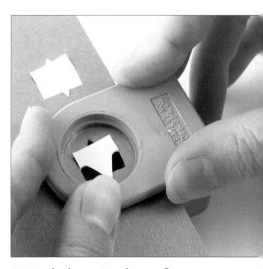

5. On a turquoise luggage label, make marks 38mm (1½in) down the length and use these as a guide to snip the corners, creating the distinctive label shape. Repeat on the other three luggage labels.

6. Place and secure the flip and fold bookmark template number 12 on scrap aqua card. Cut one shape, skip the next one and cut the third. Repeat on turquoise card.

7. Push the point down, flip it over and secure it. Place the circular craft punch around it upside down as shown, and punch to make a photo corner.

55

8. Make two photo corners in each colour and attach each one to a luggage label in the opposite colour.

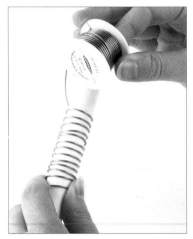

9. Take a length of 18 gauge turquoise wire, wrap it round an old plastic tube ten times and squeeze the wraps together to tighten the coil.

10. Snip off coils using wire cutters, to make jump rings.

11. Use round-nosed pliers to curl one end of each jump ring.

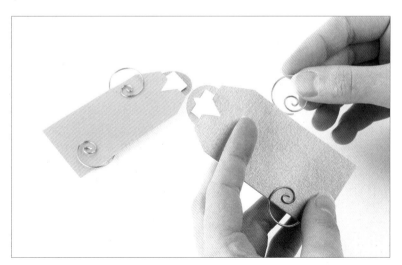

12. Clip the jump rings on to the luggage labels as shown.

13. Punch out a vellum daisy. Tear a bit of complementary coloured vellum and a bit of turquoise card, making sure you tear towards you.

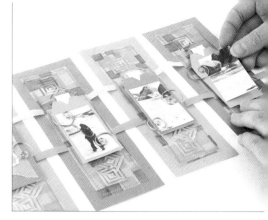

14. Layer these three items to create a collage and use a sewing machine and straight stitch to sew them to the front of a luggage label.

15. Use 3D foam squares to stick the luggage label to the tag on the far left. Tie a length of thread to a heart-shaped button and stick it to your collage with high tack glue.

16. Take a landscape-shaped photograph and cut it into strips 38mm x 63mm (1½in x 2½in). Place the strips of photograph behind the jump rings on your luggage labels.

What a wonderful way to capture a special moment or person. Folded, the tag book makes a personal keepsake. It can also be opened and framed to make a picture gift. When I look at this tag book, I can't help being taken back to the time and place where the photograph was taken, and I have used colours and embellishments to enhance these impressions. I can almost smell the sea, feel the sand underfoot and remember all the wishes I made on that magical beach in Western Australia years ago.

We all have photographs with stories to tell, stashed in shoe boxes or lost in albums. I invite you to take them out and draw inspiration from them. What colours, patterns and textures would bring them to life? Then I dare you to scour craft shops for appropriate papers, scrounge a sewing machine and spend time reliving those precious moments and framing them as they deserve.

Peel-offs

by Judy Balchin

Birthdays, anniversaries, weddings, seasonal celebrations... they are all perfect excuses for making those extra-special cards. The delight of receiving a handmade card can only be outweighed by the enjoyment to be gained from making one. These days it could not be easier, thanks to peel-off craft stickers. These sheets of stickers come in a wide range of colours and themes, are amazingly easy to use and give a truly professional finish to your cards. Your only problem will be how to choose just which of the hundreds of designs to use. Flowers, animals, borders and corners, lettering, frames, wedding and birthday designs and much more – the list seems endless!

The techniques described in the following pages take you from simply sticking through to embossing and creating sophisticated borders and corners. Cards can be simple, or they can be embellished with handmade papers and jewels. Matching gifts can be created too – these stickers may be delicate in appearance, but they are surprisingly tough. They will stick to plastic, glass and even wax, and will adhere to flat and curved surfaces. So now it is time to begin. You are about to embark on a journey of fun and creativity, and I hope you enjoy it as much as I have done. Bon voyage and happy sticking!

Judy

Simply Sticking

Simplicity is the key to this first project, and this time the phrase 'less is more' really does produce the best results. Choose pastel colours to set off the delicate lines of this classic design. In this case, a plain and simple border will emphasise, rather than detract from, the central design.

You will need
Gold floral craft sticker

Gold border craft sticker

Pink card 7cm x 12cm
(2¾ x 4¾in)

White card 18 x 15cm
(7 x 5⅞in)

Pink handmade paper
7 x 13cm (2¾ x 5⅛in)

Scalpel (pointed blade)

Rule

Pencil

Scissors

Spray adhesive

Cutting mat

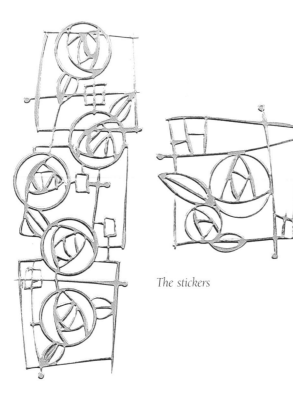

The stickers

1. Use the tip of the scalpel to lift the sticker from the backing sheet.

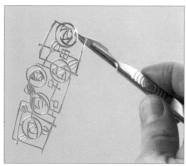

2. Let it rest for a minute to regain its original shape before sticking it to the card.

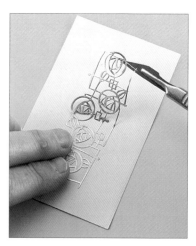

3. Lay the sticker on a piece of pale pink card and press it flat with your fingers.

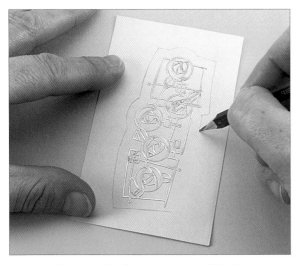

4. Lightly pencil a border 5mm (¼in) away from the edge of the sticker.

5. Using the pencilled line as a guide, cut round the sticker with a scalpel.

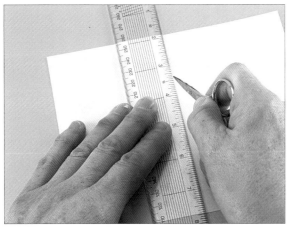

6. Pencil a line down the centre of the rectangle of white card. Score with the point of a pair of scissors and fold.

7. Tear a 5mm (¼in) strip from each edge of the piece of handmade paper.

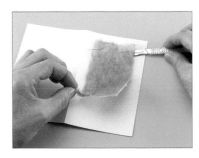

8. Spray the back of the piece of handmade paper with adhesive.

9. Position the handmade paper centrally on the front of the white card.

10. Spray the back of the pink card with adhesive and place on the handmade paper.

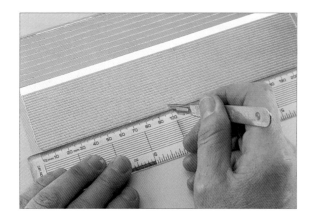

11. Use a scalpel to cut two lengths of gold craft sticker strip for the border.

12. Position the border strips across the top and bottom of the card.

13. Cut two longer pieces of gold strip and press them in place to complete the border.

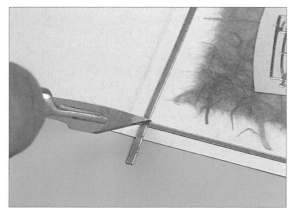

14. To neaten the corners, cut diagonally through each corner.

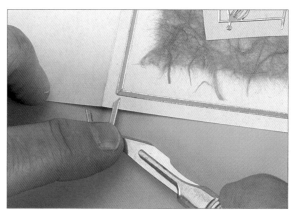

15. Remove the overhanging border pieces.

The finished card

*You will find a single motif on the craft sticker
sheet used for the card. These motifs are ideal for
creating a coordinating gift tag.*

It is the variety and positioning of the backing materials that really set off these craft stickers, so be inventive with your backgrounds and colours. In the selection shown here, the stickers are attached to lengths of ribbon, foam squares, torn handmade paper and painted acetate to create a range of very different cards.

Cutting Corners

You will find sheets of special craft stickers that are made to decorate the corners and borders of your cards. These can be used very successfully on their own to create central panels and fancy borders. Delicate handmade paper, gold filigree corners and beaded tassels combine to lend a sophisticated look to this classic card. Fancy craft scissors are used to cut the square central panel.

You will need

Gold corner craft stickers

Thin gold border sticker

Pale green card 22 x 9cm
(8⅝ x 3½in)

Pale green card 6cm (2⅜in) square

Salmon-coloured handmade paper
10 x 11cm
(3⅞ x 4¼in)

Pencil

60cm (23⅝in) length of green
embroidery thread

24 small gold beads

Needle

Double-sided adhesive pads

Fancy craft scissors

Spray adhesive

Scalpel

Cutting mat

Rule

Scissors for scoring the card

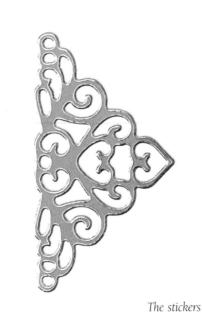

The stickers

1. Score the rectangle of green card down the centre and fold. Lightly pencil a line down the right-hand side, 2cm (¾in) in from the edge.

2. Spray the back of the handmade paper with adhesive. Press it on to the front of the card, with the right-hand side to the pencil line.

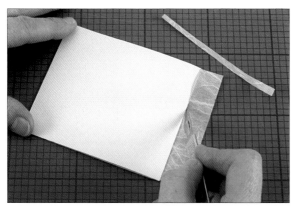

3. Press the handmade paper flat. Turn the card over and use a scalpel on a cutting mat to cut off the excess.

4. Lift a corner sticker from the backing sheet and press it on to the top edge of the green card, lining it up with the handmade paper.

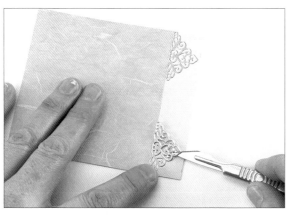

5. Press another corner sticker on to the bottom edge of the card.

6. Place a third sticker centrally along the line of the handmade paper.

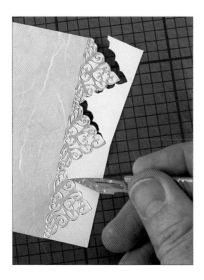

7. Open the card and cut carefully round the edges of the craft stickers with a scalpel.

8. Pencil diagonal lines and a 5mm (¼in) border round the square of green card. Cut round the border using fancy craft scissors.

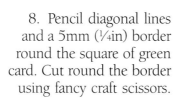

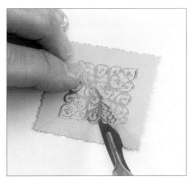

9. Lift a corner sticker with the scalpel and lay it across the diagonal on the card.

10. Lay another sticker opposite, butting the stickers together carefully.

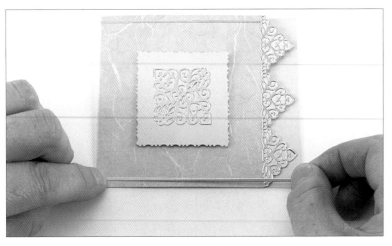

11. Fix the green square to the card using double-sided adhesive pads. Cut two lengths of border and lay them along the top and bottom edges of the card. Trim to fit.

12. Slip the embroidery thread round the fold and tie a knot, leaving trailing ends.

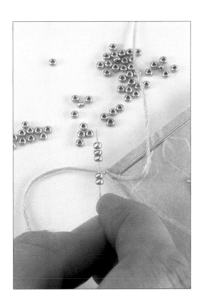

13. Using a needle, thread twelve small gold beads on to one of the trailing ends of the embroidery thread. Tie a knot about 5cm (2in) from the end of the embroidery thread and trim off the excess.

14. Repeat with the other length of thread, but tie the knot about 7cm (2¾in) from the end. Trim off the excess.

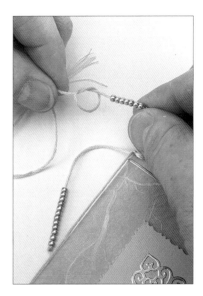

The finished card

*The classic look of this handmade card and
matching gift tag makes it ideal for a wedding
card or a special invitation.*

Corner stickers come in a variety of styles and colours. For these examples, the backing cards and materials were chosen to complement the different stickers.

To give your designs extra sparkle, use metallic card and embellish the corner motifs with gems.

Metal Magic

As craft stickers adhere to any smooth surface, why not try sticking them to metal foil and embossing them? Look for good strong designs with room for further decoration. Embossing is very easy, inexpensive and great fun. The raised appearance and jewelled embellishments are very effective, giving your finished handmade card a truly exclusive look.

You will need

Copper coloured craft sticker

Piece of thin gold foil 12cm (4¾in) square

Piece of gold card 10 x 20cm (4 x 8in)

Ballpoint pen

Scrap paper

Scissors

Strong clear adhesive

Rule

Set square

Pencil

1 x 8mm amber gem

4 x 6mm amber gems

The sticker

1. Lift the sticker from the backing paper and lay it on the square of gold foil.

2. Lift the circular central motif and place it on the gold foil square.

3. Turn the foil over and rub it with your finger to reveal the design in relief.

4. Make a pad of scrap paper and lay the foil on it. Use the ballpoint pen to emboss a ring of dots around the two central circles.

5. Work round the design, embossing lines of dots around the decorative border.

6. Turn the foil over and check that all the embossed dots show through on the right side.

7. Use a rule and set square to measure and draw a 9cm (3½in) square round the design.

8. Turn the design over. Working from the central design to the square border, draw in swirls and wavy lines.

9. Cut out the embossed gold square.

10. Score and fold the rectangle of gold card. Spread the back of the foil with strong adhesive.

11. Decorate the motif with the gems, fixing them in place with spots of strong adhesive.

The finished card

Dots and swirls of embossing work well with this copper
sticker and gold card. The gift tag is a simpler, but
equally effective, version of the larger card.

Embossed work can be simple or intricate, to give a modern or a traditional look to your cards. Mix and match gold, silver and black craft stickers with silver and gold foils, and try adding a few faceted gems here and there for an extra sparkle.

78

Embroidery

by Dorothy Wood

For me, one of the nicest things to happen on a birthday, anniversary or other special occasion is to receive a card and, although there are lots of lovely cards in the shops, it is always that bit more special if the card is handmade too.

I love making cards myself and, because I am also mad about embroidery and textiles, like to use fabrics and stitches to make pretty, tactile designs. Although I prefer very contemporary, simple designs, it is essential to match the card to the person, so I have created a range of cards using a variety of embroidery techniques and styles that would be suitable to send to family, friends and colleagues.

You can stitch the designs that follow in any order, but if you are new to embroidery use these pages as a mini embroidery workshop, building on your skills and learning new techniques in easy stages. My festive star design shows you how to achieve a stunning effect with simple straight stitching on paper. In the other projects I introduce new stitches such as French knots, lazy daisy stitch and chain stitch, and also show how decorative buttons can add a different dimension to stitching.

To give the cards a contemporary feel, I have drawn on the plethora of paper crafting techniques using translucent paper, eyelets and decorative paperclips and buttons to complement the embroidery designs.

I hope you enjoy making the cards as much as I have and are inspired to create some designs of your own.

Happy stitching.

Festive Star

Stitching on paper

Simple straight stitches can be used to create a variety of intricate thread patterns and motifs. In this elegant design, straight and back stitches are used to form a star shape which is then embellished with sequins. The combination of translucent parchment paper and metallic card is particularly effective for Christmas designs.

You will need

Silver card, 10cm (4in) square

Mouse (or foam) mat

Masking tape

Dressmaker's pin

Paper scissors

Embroidery scissors

Parchment paper, 10cm (4in) square

Silver gel pen

Double-sided tape

Silver metallic thread

No. 9 crewel needle

Star-shaped silver sequins

Single-fold, white hammer-finish card, A6 (4 x 6in)

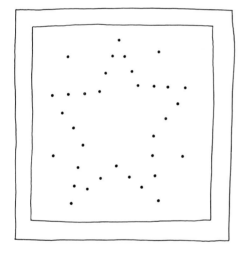

Full-size template

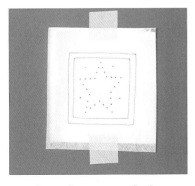

1. Place the piece of silver card on the mouse mat, then secure the template on top with masking tape.

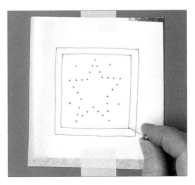

2. Prick holes through each dot on the star, the four sequin holes and at each corner of the inner square.

3. Remove the template, then, using the holes as a guide, trim the piece of silver card to the size of the inner square.

4. Secure the parchment paper on top of the silver card, then use the silver gel pen to draw a square about 5mm (³/₁₆in) away from the edges of the silver card.

5. Prick holes through the parchment paper in the same places as the silver card.

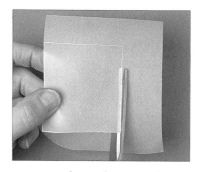

6. Trim along the outside edge of the silver line.

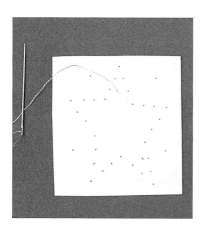

7. Thread a length of silver metallic thread on the needle, then use double-sided tape to anchor the tail end on the back of the silver card adjacent to hole 1 (see thread stitching template).

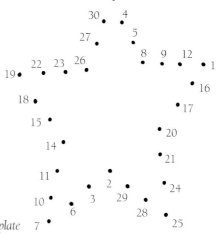

Thread stitching template

8. Place the parchment paper on top of the silver card and line up the holes. Bring the needle up through hole 1 on the template and down through hole 2.

9. Bring the needle up through hole 3 and down through hole 4.

10. Carry on taking the thread through consecutive holes until the design is complete. Anchor the thread on the back of the card with double-sided tape and trim off the excess.

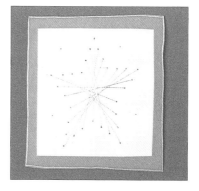

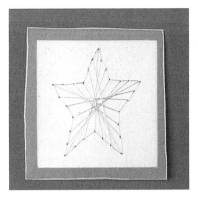

11. Anchor a second length of metallic thread, bring it out through hole 1, then take the needle down through hole 4 to start the back stitch outline of the star shape.

12. Bring the thread up through hole 5 and back down through hole 4.

13. Continue working round the edge of the star in this way to create a solid line of back stitch. Anchor the thread on the back of the silver card.

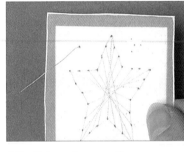

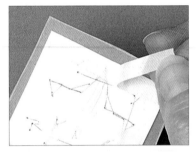

14. Secure another metallic thread on the back of the silver card and bring it up through one of the sequin holes. Pick up a sequin, let it drop down to the card, then stitch back through the paper and card at the bottom of the valley between two points of the star.

15. Bring the needle up through the centre of the sequin and down through the next-but-one valley. Repeat with a third stitch to secure the sequin. Attach the other sequins in the same way.

16. Stick three pieces of double-sided tape on the back of the silver card and peel off the backing strips.

17. Carefully position the embroidered design on to the front of the white card to complete the project.

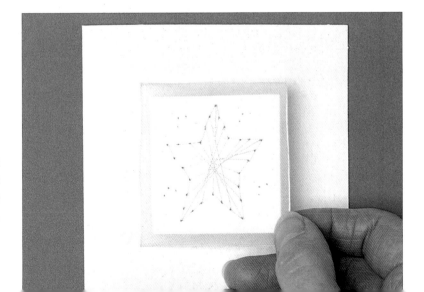

The finished card

Tip
Use bright colours of metallic thread, sequins and gel pens to make bold, colourful Christmas cards.

All of these Christmas motif cards were made in a similar manner to the card shown on pages 82–85, using a variety of metallic threads on different translucent and metallic papers.

To make your own stitched cards, draw out the design on paper, mark in the thread lines, then work out the order you need to stitch!

The Christmas tree and snowflake designs are quite easy to stitch, but you will get better, more accurate results if you draw templates on graph paper. Embellish the finished designs with white frosted seed beads, which can be stitched to the card or attached with tiny dots of glitter glue.

The winter tree design is stitched on 'white frost' parchment paper and flat translucent sequins are added as you stitch. Stitch the long branch lines first and then tuck the sequins under the thread before sewing in place with the shorter branch lines. The finished design is attached to the card using tiny 2mm ($^1/_{16}$in) eyelets.

The stitching sequence for the gold star card is slightly more complicated to work out, so I have included a thread stitching template (below).

To complement the cards, you could make some small gift tags using a simple stitch motif similar to the card design. Cut a piece of card to size and then mount the design on it.

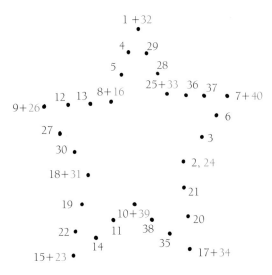

Thread stitching template for the gold star card. Start by bringing the thread out through hole 1, down through hole 2, up through hole 3, etc. The holes at the points of the star and those in the valleys between the points are used twice.

Topiary Tree

Stitching with buttons

Some decorative buttons are specially designed to use in embroidery and these can be very inspiring when designing cards. This topiary tree, for example, looks quite majestic in its large terracotta pot. Clusters of French knots form the oranges, stem stitch is used for the tree trunk and a variation of lazy daisy stitch, known as filled chain stitch, forms the leaves.

You will need
Cream Panama fabric

Cotton backing fabric

Low-loft wadding

Masking tape

Double-sided tape

Water-soluble marker and water sprayer

Two-fold, rectangular-aperture, orange card, A6 (4 x 6in)

Ruler

Embroidery hoop

No. 9 crewel needle

Six-stranded embroidery cotton (pale and dark tones of orange and green and brown)

Embroidery scissors

Terracotta pot button and four small buttons

Full-size template

1. Secure the fabric over the template, then use a water-soluble marker to trace the design.

2. Open the card, position the aperture centrally over the traced design and carefully mark its four corners on the fabric.

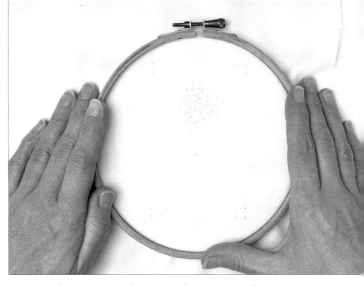

3. Draw a rectangle round the four points, then draw four lines approximately 6mm (¹/₄in) in from the marks.

4. Lay the inner embroidery hoop on a flat surface, place the backing fabric and the marked fabric on top, then fit the outer hoop.

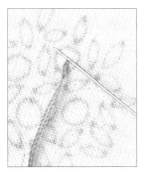

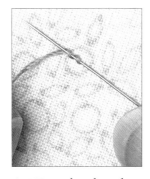

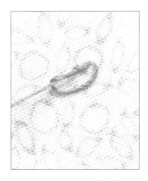

5. Work up the oranges with French knots. Using two strands of pale orange thread, bring the needle out in one of the marked circles. Take a tiny stitch next to where the thread emerged but leave the needle in the fabric.

6. Wrap the thread around the point of the needle two or three times . . .

7. . . . then pull the needle through.

8. When the knot is tight, take the needle back through the fabric close to the knot.

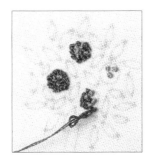

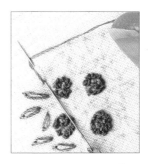

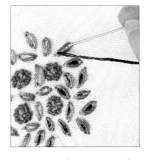

9. Work several pale orange French knots in each circle, then fill in the rest of the circles with dark orange French knots.

10. Use two strands of pale green cotton to work a single chain stitch for each leaf (see page 95).

11. Use three strands of dark green cotton to work a straight stitch down the centre of each leaf. The finished stitch is known as filled chain stitch.

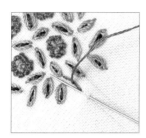

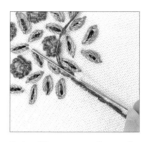

12. Using one strand of two tones of brown, bring the needle out at the top of the trunk. Work a 6mm (¹/₄in) straight stitch bringing the needle back out 3mm (¹/₈in) away from where the thread first emerged.

13. Work another 6mm straight stitch and bring the needle out at the end of the first stitch. Continue down to the bottom of the trunk and sew in the thread end.

14. Use new thread to work a second row of stem stitch so that there is no fabric showing between.

15. Continue with more rows of stem stitch until the trunk is completely filled.

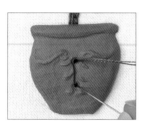

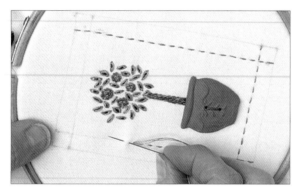

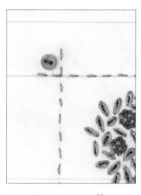

16. Use brown thread to sew on the button. Take the thread through the holes several times, then secure the thread on the reverse side with two tiny back stitches.

17. Work a row of running stitch along one of the marked lines around the topiary tree. Try to keep the stitches the same size and end a stitch at the cross point of the lines. Work along the other lines, keeping the stitches the same length and in the same position, especially where the lines cross.

18. Sew a small round button in each corner of the design.

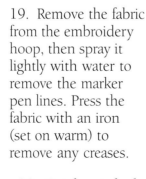

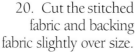

19. Remove the fabric from the embroidery hoop, then spray it lightly with water to remove the marker pen lines. Press the fabric with an iron (set on warm) to remove any creases.

20. Cut the stitched fabric and backing fabric slightly over size.

21. Cut a piece of low-loft wadding the same size as the aperture in the card.

22. Open up the card, lay it face down on the work surface and apply strips of double-sided tape as shown. Remove the backing paper from the four strips round the aperture.

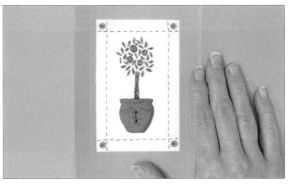

23. Lay the stitched fabric face up on the work surface and carefully position the card on top. Press down to secure the double-sided tape.

24. Turn the card over, place the wadding on the stitched fabric and remove the backing from the other strips of double-sided tape.

25. Fold the front flap over so that it just catches on the strips of double-sided tape at the top and bottom of the card.

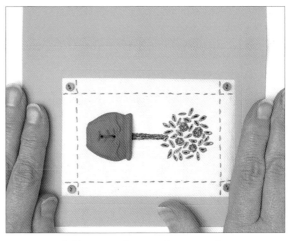

26. Carefully turn the card over, taking care not to disturb the wadding, then apply pressure to secure all the double-sided tape.

Tip
When using large
buttons, you might find it
useful to use small glue
dots or silicone adhesive
to stick them to the fabric
before stitching them
in place.

Opposite
Buttons for embroidery come in all shapes and sizes, and the embroidery
around the button can be as easy or complicated as you like. To make a
very simple card, choose a large heart button and use very basic stitches to
create the pretty design. You can use appliqué to change areas of the
background colour before stitching; the 'grass' in the birdhouse design, for
example, looks like fabric paint but is simply appliquéd organza.

Be My Valentine

Stitching on felt

Felt is a super material to use for simple embroidered cards as it does not fray and can be cut to any shape or size. Felt is thick enough to be used without a backing fabric as the thread can be anchored invisibly on the back. This pretty design introduces chain stitch and lazy daisy stitch, and it is worked in an attractive variegated cotton. The three strands of cotton are separated and each worked as a single thread (which is similar in thickness to No. 8 coton perlé).

Tip
When using variegated cotton cut particular colour areas along the length to highlight features such as the centre flower in the heart design.

You will need
Purple felt, 10 x 12cm (4 x 5in)
Lightweight tracing paper
Pencil
Dressmaker's pins
Three-ply, pima cotton
(variegated sky blue and pink)
No. 9 crewel needle
Single-fold, lilac card, A6 (4 x 6in)

Embroidery scissors
Pinking shears
Masking tape

One pink and four lilac snaps
Hole punch, setting tool, setting mat
and hammer

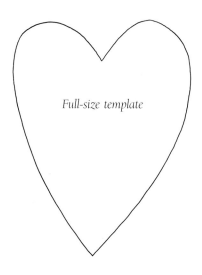

Full-size template

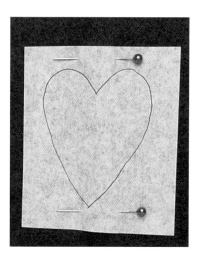

1. Trace the solid outline of the heart shape from the template on to lightweight tracing paper, then pin the traced motif in the middle of the piece of felt.

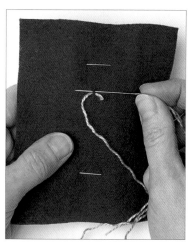

2. Separate a single strand of cotton, thread a length on a needle, then secure the tail end on the back of the felt with a tiny back stitch.

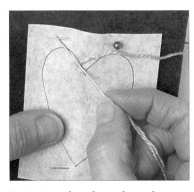

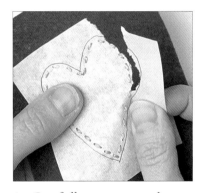

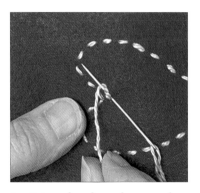

3. Bring the thread to the front, then, sewing through the paper and felt, work a row of running stitch just inside the marked line.

4. Carefully tear away the paper around the outside of the heart shape, then lift out the centre piece.

5. Bring the thread up at the valley of the heart shape and work a row of chain stitch. Make a small stitch from the start point, loop the thread under the needle . . .

6. . . . then pull the needle and thread through to close the loop.

7. Make the next small stitch from within the loop of the previous stitch. Repeat steps 6–7 round and down to the bottom of the heart.

8. When you reach the bottom point of the heart shape, anchor the last loop of the chain stitch by taking the thread down through the felt just outside the loop.

9. Work chain stitch up the other side of the heart shape, then work two rows of back stitch, one inside and one outside the existing stitching. Complete the border by working single chain stitches (also known as lazy daisy stitches) around the outer row of back stitch. Space the stitches evenly – say between pairs of back stitches.

10. Using a pink length of the thread, work five single chain stitches to form a flower in the centre of the heart motif. Leave a 3mm ($\frac{1}{8}$in) gap in the centre so that a snap can be inserted later on.

11. Fill the area around the flower with random running stitches – a technique which is known as seeding.

12. Use lengths of masking tape to mark the finished size of the felt, then use pinking shears to cut the felt to shape.

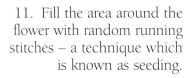

Tip
Take care to match the teeth of the pinking shears with the cut zigzag edge to ensure that the pattern is continuous.

13. Place the felt on the setting mat, then use the hole punch head of the setting tool and the hammer to make a hole in the centre of the flower.

14. Insert a pink snap in the hole, turn the felt over on to the setting mat, then use the other heads of the setting tool to set the snap.

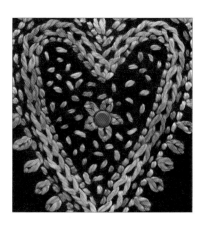

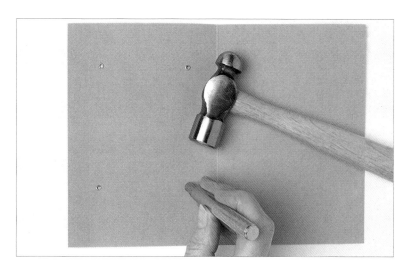

15. Open the card (face up) on the setting mat, position the embroidered felt on the right-hand side then punch a hole through all layers in each corner of the felt. Insert the snaps through the holes, carefully turn the card over, then set the snaps to complete the project.

The finished card

Tip

You could use the same stitches with different motifs to make a series of cards for a variety of occasions. Choose a variegated thread that tones with the felt and the card for best effect.

These pretty designs look quite different to the 'Be my Valentine' card but actually use all the same stitches. The contemporary look to the cards is achieved by using printed vellum paper available from scrapbook suppliers. As well as stripes, the paper is available in checks and polka dots in a range of colours. The small felt motifs, which are stitched on larger pieces of felt then pressed and trimmed to size, can be used to make a whole range of cards and gift tags.

To make the printed vellum stand out on the matching card colour, tear a square of white paper slightly smaller than the vellum paper. Attach the felt squares with simple stitches or eyelets, through both types of paper and then stick the finished design to the front of the card with double-sided sticky tape.

Matching gift tags are easy to make using just one of the little felt squares.

Plan your designs by drawing the squares and rectangles on paper and then use these as a cutting template.

Using Punches

by Julie Hickey

I can't remember when my love affair with punches began. I was always an avid stamper, and I used to think that punches were only for making animal shapes such as rabbits. Then I was introduced to the daisy punch, and I was totally hooked!

I love the simplicity of punched cards: the variety of effects that you can create by using different papers and cards, and the fact that you can mix them with wire, beads and threads to give added interest.

There is so much that you can do with just a square punch: you can use the squares to mount on to or create a simple square or a rectangular aperture. You can then use another punch to punch the square waste from a card, creating a square with a shaped hole in it.

There are so many different punches available now, and I feel sure that whether you are a punch addict or just embarking on your journey of discovery, you will find many hints and tips to help you get more from your punches.

Use the following pages to get your creativity flowing and create your own fabulous punched greetings cards.

Basic techniques

Punches are very versatile: you do not have to use them just for the shape that they punch. A square punch can create square or rectangular apertures in cards, or punched squares or diamonds for layering other shapes on to. You can punch out different shapes and use the square punch upside down around the hole to create a square with a shaped hole in it.

You will need
Card and card blanks
Square punch
Heart-shaped punch
Double-sided tape

Making a square aperture

1. Work with the card open. Put the punch in from the top, as far as it will go. Judge by eye that the punch is in the middle of the card, or use a set square to measure it.

2. Make a second aperture at the bottom of the card, in the same way.

3. You can not punch out a third square in the middle, as the punch will not reach that far. Punch out a square in a different colour and place it in the middle of the card as shown. Stick it in place with double-sided tape.

Making a rectangular aperture

1. Work with the card open. Put the square punch in from the side and line up the top of the card with the edge of the punch. Push the punch in as far as it will go and punch.

Tip
When using the punch upside down, push down gently until you feel the punch bite, position your paper or card, then push all the way down to punch out the shape.

2. Line the punch up in the same way at the bottom of the card and punch out another square.

3. Punch two overlapping squares in the middle of the card to finish the long aperture.

Making a three aperture card

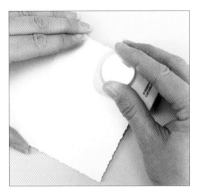

1. Open the card. Line up the small square punch with the top of the card and punch out a square.

2. Do the same at the bottom of the card.

3. Centre the punch between the two apertures by eye and punch out the middle square.

Making an opening card with a punch

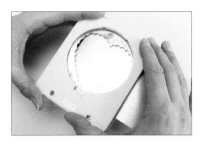

1. Fold a piece of paper and place it in the upside-down punch, so that you can see clearly where the punch will cut the shape.

2. Make sure that the fold in the paper is inside the punch area. Here the fold can just be seen on the left-hand side of the heart shape.

3. When the shape is punched, the fold will remain intact, and the shape will open out to make a gift tag or small card.

Using the waste

1. Punch out a daisy and keep the waste paper out of which it has been punched. The punched out daisy itself can be used for another card.

2. Hold a square punch upside down and feed in the waste paper. I have marked the centre points on the metal underside of my punch. Line the daisy petals up with the marks.

3. Punch out the square. The daisy-shaped hole will be centred in the middle of the square.

Border punches

1. Place the paper in the border punch. Make sure it is pushed in and lines up with the back plate, and punch. Move the punched strip along and line it up with the pattern on the base of the punch. Punch again, line up again and punch until the whole strip is punched out.

2. When you have completed your border, pull off the waste paper edge.

3. You can cut strips of paper in different widths and use the border punch on both sides, as shown. I have found that a 3cm (1¼in) strip works well, but by altering the width you can achieve different looks.

The finished panel

Sponging through a stencil

1. Punch a flower shape out of card to make a stencil. Many punches are great for creating stencils. Have fun discovering which shapes work best.

2. Position the stencil on your card, and using a piece of cosmetic sponge and an inkpad, sponge through the stencil.

Here are some of the beautiful effects you can achieve using punches with the techniques shown.

Leafy Luggage Labels

I love these copper tones, combined with the rich lustre of the green card. You will learn how to use the waste from an oak leaf punch to create a rectangular shape with a hole in it, then how to transform this rectangle into a tag, adding a wire flourish. You will also use your punches to make stencils, and sponge through them to decorate the background of your card. Leaf cards make great masculine cards.

You will need

Oak leaf and rectangle punches

3mm (¹/₈in) hole punch

22g copper wire and wire cutters

Round-nosed pliers

Copper card blank, 12cm (4¾in) square

Emerald sparkle card and scrap card for stencil

3D foam squares

Scissors

Set square

Pearlescent ivy inkpad

Cosmetic sponge

1. Punch out a leaf shape from a piece of scrap card, to make a stencil.

2. Use a piece of cosmetic sponge and a green inkpad to sponge through the stencil onto the copper card blank. Place the leaf shapes randomly, upside down too, and make sure that some go off the edge of the card, for a natural look.

4. Place the rectangle punch upside down around the punched-out leaf, and punch.

3. Punch leaves out of emerald sparkle card, leaving plenty of space between each leaf.

5. Cut away the part of the card with the rectangle punched out of it. This allows the punch to go into the card and align the next punch. This is a way of using the waste.

6. Punch two more rectangles in the same way. Then use the 3mm ($^1/_8$ in) hole punch to punch a hole in the top of each rectangle.

7. Snip the top corners of each rectangle to create a luggage label shape.

8. Thread a length of copper wire through the hole in a luggage label. Use round-nosed pliers to start to coil the end, then use your fingers to shape it. Twist the wire over, then trim the other side with wire cutters and shape it in the same way.

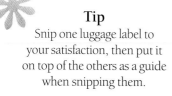

Tip
Snip one luggage label to your satisfaction, then put it on top of the others as a guide when snipping them.

9. Place 3D foam squares to the back of the luggage labels.

10. Position the luggage labels on the stencilled card using a set square. Place the middle label first.

Rich colours and shapes from the natural world are perfectly set off by the luggage label motif in this simple but effective card.

More leafy wonders to inspire you to change the look while using the same punch. The colours are all variations on a natural theme, from soft pearl greens through to the rich lustre of dark copper. The card on the bottom left combines delicate vellum papers with pearlescent card and oak leaf punches in different sizes.

Silk Painting

by Mandy Southan

Silk painting is a wonderful medium for both large- and small-scale work, and lends itself perfectly to greetings cards. Painted silk cards are easy and fun to make, and the jewel-like colours and luxurious sheen of the fabric make them look very special and eye-catching.

If you have never done any silk painting before you will be surprised how fascinating it is, and greetings cards are ideal first projects. You will not need a lot of expensive equipment, and cards are small enough to complete very quickly. The designs which follow will introduce you to basic silk painting techniques and materials, with designs which you can copy or adapt. It is lovely to design your own cards for special friends, but do not worry if you cannot draw: you can trace from books or magazines, use your own photographs, or just make up abstract patterns like some of the ones featured in this book.

If you have some experience of silk painting, you will find that painting cards gives you an excellent opportunity to enjoy yourself playing with new materials and trying out different designs and colour combinations. There are lots of new and exciting products which can add an extra dimension to your designs – try adding texture and shimmer with glitter liners, metallic paints and foils. There are endless ways of combining new materials with traditional silk painting techniques: in terms of possibilities, each project featured is only the tip of the iceberg!

The projects on the following pages were all painted with colours mixed from six basic hues. The materials list tells you which were used for each project. Colour mixing takes practice; experiment by making up your own colourways and above all, enjoy the beautiful colours that will appear as if by magic as the paints spread and blend on the silk. I think you will gain as much pleasure from painting silk greetings cards as your friends and family will from receiving them.

Mandy Southan

Opposite
A selection of handmade silk painted greetings cards.

Butterfly

This project is a good one to start with, as you only need three colours of paint and you do not even need a frame. It uses a very simple technique: the silk is folded before applying the colours so a symmetrical pattern is created when it is unfolded. The colours run along the creases, resembling the veins in a butterfly's wing.

   The painted silk can be stuck on to a pre-cut shaped card, as shown in the project, and the surplus silk trimmed off. Alternatively, you can stick the painted silk on to an oblong of white card, then trace the butterfly shape given below on the back of the card. If you do this, the folded card and the silk can both be cut out at the same time, using a sharp craft knife or scissors.

You will need

Butterfly-shaped card or white card plus template

Piece of Habotai silk slightly larger than the template

Polythene sheet

Craft knife

Scissors

Silk colours: I used golden yellow, magenta and ultramarine blue, plus violet mixed from magenta and ultramarine blue

Brush No. 6

Iron and ironing board or pad

Two small coins or weights

Spray adhesive

place to fold   *place to fold*

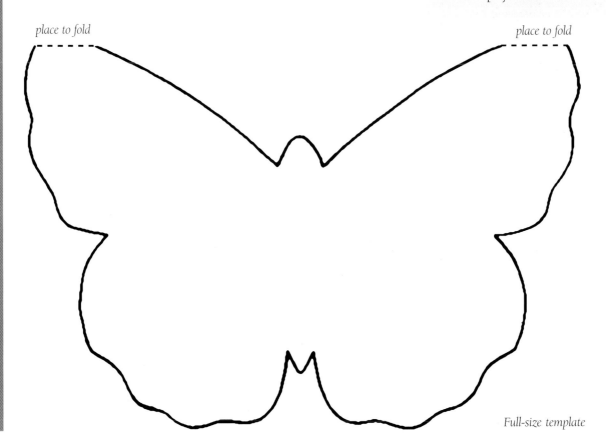

Full-size template

114

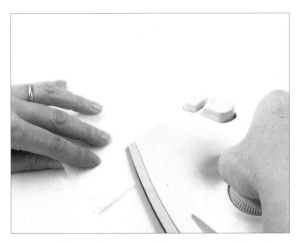

1. Protect your work surface with polythene. Cut a piece of silk a little larger than the template. The silk should be placed with the right (slightly shinier) side upwards.

2. Switch on the iron. Place your work right side down on a pad of cotton material or an ironing board. Pick up the nearest corners and fold the silk upwards. Press in the crease.

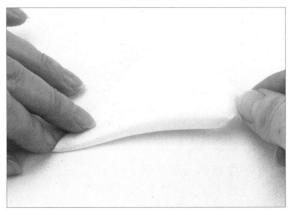

3. Fold the crease you have just ironed in upwards so the silk is folded into quarters. Press in the crease again.

4. Repeat the process, folding the silk upwards and into eighths to make a narrow triangle. Press in the crease again.

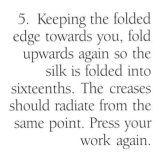

5. Keeping the folded edge towards you, fold upwards again so the silk is folded into sixteenths. The creases should radiate from the same point. Press your work again.

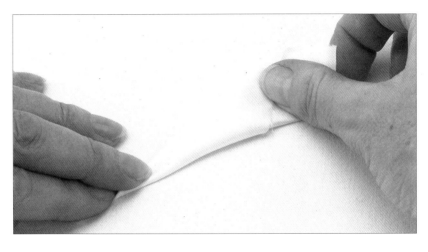

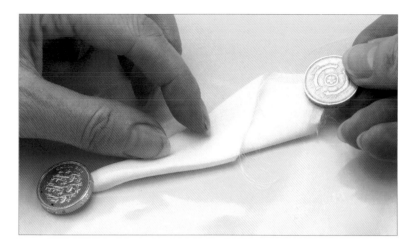

6. Protect your work surface with the polythene sheet and transfer the folded cone of silk to it carefully. Weight the ends so it does not unfold. Coins are ideal for this.

7. Using a dropper, drop the colours you plan to use into individual palettes, mixing colours and diluting them if necessary. Test the colours on a piece of scrap silk.

8. With a No. 6 brush and beginning with yellow, apply colour generously to the end of the cone. Use a dabbing motion to ensure that it penetrates the layers of silk.

9. Make sure the yellow has spread under the coin, right to the point. Rinse the brush and dry it on absorbent paper. Working quickly and dabbing as before, add magenta next to the yellow, overlapping the edges of the yellow a little.

10. Repeat with blue, then finish with violet.

11. Use the end of a clean brush to lift the silk carefully. Check that the colours have penetrated the silk and apply more if necessary. Leave your work to dry folded.

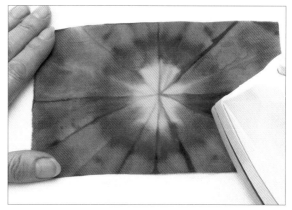

12. Unfold the silk and iron it flat. This will fix iron-fix paints.

13. Protect your work surface with paper. Lay the silk on the paper with the right side down and spray it lightly and evenly with adhesive. Position the card template carefully on the back of the painted silk, so that the centre of the butterfly's body aligns with its centre fold.

14. Turn the silk over and smooth out any air bubbles or creases with your fingertips. Leave it to dry for a few minutes.

15. Cut carefully round the template. The spray adhesive will stop the silk fraying.

Opposite
A collection of butterflies ready to take flight

The finished card

Magic Carpet

This richly coloured silk card has a touch of Eastern promise, and is perfect for a festive greeting to a friend. The edges of the silk are fringed to make it look like a little carpet before you stick it to the card.

This project uses a glitter pen, which not only adds sparkle to your painted silk but also acts as a resist, preventing the colours spreading to adjoining areas. The silk is painted with blended colours and allowed to dry before applying the glitter, which is supported in a clear medium, so that it lies over coloured rather than white silk. Finally, sections of the work are over-painted using a darker shade, which changes the background subtly as it moves across them.

You will need

Piece of Habotai silk large enough to pin to a frame

3B pencil

Frame

Silk pins

Silk colours: I used golden yellow; magenta; ultramarine blue, and a violet shade mixed from ultramarine and magenta

Brushes Nos. 6 and 8

Glitter outliner

Two-fold oblong white watercolour card for mounting the silk

Spray adhesive

Scissors

Full-size template

Tip

You can make up your own designs by drawing with the glitter pens directly on to the dry, blended background. This spontaneous approach saves the time that is spent tracing on a design and outlining it carefully, and is very useful if you want to make a large batch of cards.

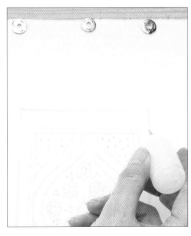

1. Pencil the design on to the silk fairly heavily, so it shows through the background colours. Pin to the frame and apply gutta to the outer edge only.

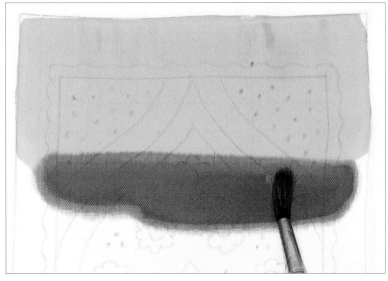

2. Allow the gutta to dry. Mix up the paints you will need. Using a No. 8 brush, sweep yellow paint across the fabric, followed at once by magenta.

3. Rinse the brush, dab it dry and, working quickly, use it to blend the two colours briskly so there is no hard line.

Tip

Position the silk carefully so that the grain lies straight along the edges of the design, or it will not fringe evenly.

If the silk starts to wrinkle while you are painting it, remove pins where necessary and re-tension it.

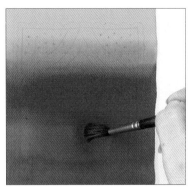

4. Quickly rinse the brush and apply violet, blending as before. Leave to dry.

5. Apply the glitter outliner over the pencil lines of your design. Leave to dry.

6. Paint over sections of the design as shown (left and below) with ultramarine and a No. 6 brush. Touch paint into the chosen sections and between the dots, allowing it to spread to the outliner. Iron-fix the silk (see page 117).

7. Trim the gutta edge from the silk using sharp scissors.

8. Pull out threads of the silk, a few at a time, to make a fringe at one end.

9. Repeat with the other end, making the fringes about 10mm (³/₈ in) deep.

10. Mount the design on the card with spray adhesive, so there is a slightly deeper border of card at the bottom.

11. Smooth down the design, working from the middle outwards and stroking down the fringe with a fingertip.

Opposite
The finished card

Magic carpets

The number of possible variations is limited only by your imagination. This design lends itself perfectly to gift tags and bookmarks. The two cards at the bottom of the photograph show designs made with bold strokes of glitter paint, brushed freely on to the painted silk.

With Love

Paint a special card for someone you love. This project uses gold outliner as a resist which blocks the silk fibres and prevents colours spreading to adjoining areas. Shading and blending the colours in the rose petals creates a three-dimensional effect. The metallic outliner prevents the silk from fraying, giving a neat edge to the design.

This design can be adapted for a wedding or birthday using silver or pearlised outliner and varying the colours, or make your own design by tracing a favourite flower from a plant catalogue. Designs can be enlarged on a photocopier.

You will need

Piece of Habotai silk large enough to pin to a frame

Frame

Silk pins

3B pencil

Brush No. 6

Gold outliner

Silk colours: I used red; the same red diluted with water or diffusing medium to make pink; three different shades of green mixed from lemon yellow and cyan; magenta, and mauve mixed from ultramarine and red

Large two-fold white card mount

Spray adhesive

The template for the card shown at 80 percent of full size – enlarge on a photocopier.

126

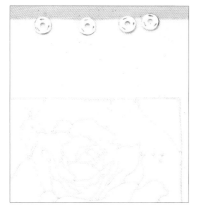

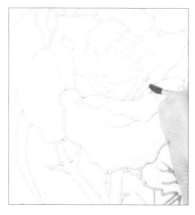

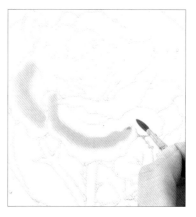

1. Trace the design lightly on the silk with a pencil. Attach to a frame. Outline carefully with gold, and leave to dry.

2. Apply plain water to the edges of the petals on the main rose, where you want the effect to be very pale.

3. Paint in the pink shade next to the plain water so it begins to blend.

4. Working quickly, paint in the darker red next to the pink. Leave some of the frilly edges white.

5. Blend in more of the darker red to shade the petals further if necessary.

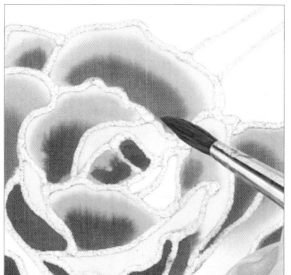

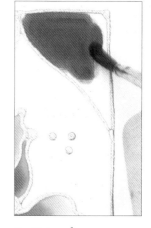

6. Touch in the centre of the rosebud. Blend the shades carefully with the tip of a clean, slightly damp brush.

7. Paint the upper corners of the design with red.

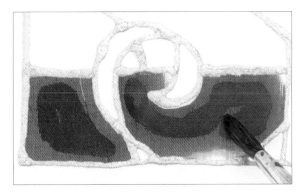

8. Paint in the lower panels with red and the lower corners with magenta.

9. Use water to damp down the ribbon and heart shapes that will be painted wet-in-wet.

10. Paint in the ribbons and hearts using magenta, leaving white spaces for highlights. Paint in the light green sections of leaves, the stalk and the bud.

11. Paint the brighter green sections of the leaves.

12. Add brighter green accents to the stalk and bud.

13. Put in the third green to shade the leaves.

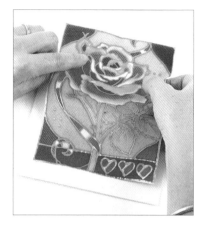

15. Iron-fix the silk (see page 117). Cut round the outer edge of gold outliner to leave a fine gold border. Mount on to a large, two-fold white card using spray adhesive.

14. Paint in the background. Leave to dry.

The finished card

A bunch of roses

*Varying the colours of the flowers
and backgrounds can produce
some very different effects.*

Glass Painting

by Judy Balchin

Handmade greetings cards and gift tags are always fun to make and a delight to receive. Many of my relatives and friends have actually framed cards that I have made, which is a compliment to me as well as a continuing pleasure for them.

The title of this chapter may seem a little worrying, so let me explain: no glass is actually used for the cards featured. I show you how glass painting techniques can be used on clear acetate, which is then mounted on, or framed by, card. It is an inexpensive way to sample the delights of this fascinating hobby.

Both designs are simple and use bold outlines . Vibrant, transparent colours make up the cat's stripes whilst the snowman sparkles in glittery ice white. The techniques can be adapted to create fridge magnets, mobiles or bookmarks, or worked on glass to make pictures, decorate plates and vases, and much more.

Part of the fun of creating your own masterpiece is browsing through the wonderful array of backing cards and papers available, and choosing coloured gems, glitter or other items for decoration. You can keep your cards simple, or make them as ornate as your imagination allows. My main problem is knowing just when to stop!

Try combining elements, taking a border from here, a motif from there, to create a new design. Do not discard ideas as you experiment with the outliners and paints: what can at first seem a mistake may spark off something new and exciting. I hope that by sharing my techniques and flights of fancy, I have provided a launch pad for your own ideas. Glass painting is both therapeutic and addictive. I should know: I have been doing it for ten years and am still enjoying every minute. My best advice is to enjoy your hobby. Have fun!

Judy

Opposite
A selection of handmade glass painted cards.

Crazy Cat

Vibrant colours and the addition of wobbly eyes gives this cat a humorous, quirky appearance which will definitely bring a smile to the face of the recipient. Animals are a fun subject, and as your confidence increases you might even decide to base a card on a favourite pet.

To begin with, you may find it helpful to photocopy the design from the book. Cut it to size and tape it to a piece of thick card. Acetate sheet tends to warp slightly when the outliner and paints are applied, so tape it down over the design before you start to make sure your working surface is completely flat.

You will need

Thick white card

Yellow card 8 x 9.5cm
(3¼ x 3¾in)

Green card 18 x 10.5cm
(7 x 4⅛in)

Acetate sheet 9 x 10cm
(3½ x 4⅛in)

Black outliner

Glass paint: red and yellow

Brush No. 4

Plastic 'wobbly' eyes x 2

Small, pointed scissors

Masking tape

Spray adhesive

Rule or straight edge

Newspaper

Full-size template

- Hold the outliner tube firmly between thumb and forefinger and squeeze gently.

Using outliner

- Wipe the nozzle frequently with absorbent paper to keep it clean.

- To produce straight lines, try the 'touch, lift and pull' technique: touch the acetate gently with the tip, squeeze the tube, then lift the tip off the surface and pull it along, a bit like icing a cake!

- If the tube starts to 'ooze', squeeze it gently on either side of the top to stop the flow.

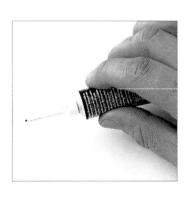

Before you begin

To make sure the acetate is grease-free, wipe it all over using absorbent paper dampened with methylated spirit or lighter fuel.

1. Place the design on thick card. Cover it with the piece of acetate and tape it flat using masking tape.

2. Carefully squeeze on two blobs of outliner where the eyes will be positioned.

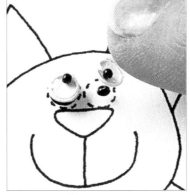

3. While the outliner is still wet, place a small plastic 'wobbly' eye on each blob and press it gently into place. Picking up the eye will be easier if you moisten your fingertip first.

4. Beginning at the top and working downwards to prevent smudging, outline the cat carefully. Leave your work to dry.

5. Lift the masking tape and carefully remove the template.

135

6. Paint in the yellow head, taking care to paint around the eyes, then the yellow stripes, legs and paws.

7. Paint in the red ears, stripes and tail. Leave your work to dry on a flat surface.

8. Cut round the edge of the cat with small sharp scissors.

9. Lay the cat face down on a piece of newspaper and cover with spray adhesive.

10. Press the cat into the centre of the rectangle of yellow card.

11. Use a cutting board, rule and the points of scissors to score down the centre of the rectangle of green card.

12. Coat the back of the yellow card with spray adhesive and press firmly to the front of the green card.

The finished card
*The head of the cat has been used for
the matching gift tag.*

Templates

gift tags

Templates on this page are shown full size.

Seasonal Greetings

To give this card a really frosty feel, I sprinkled glitter on to opaque glass paint before it dried. Then the painted acetate was mounted on 3-D effect holographic card, which shimmers through the design. The snowman's hat and scarf may look tricky, but are fiddly rather than complicated. If you do not want to paint in such small areas, the scarf and hatband can be completed in one solid colour.

You will need

Acetate sheet 9 x 13cm
(3½ x 5¼in)

Holographic card 9 x 13cm
(3½ x 5¼in)

Blue mirror card 20 x 14cm
(8¼ x 5½in)

Outliners: black and white

Glass paints: white, red, turquoise, orange, yellow, green, purple and clear

Glitter

Masking tape

Brush No.4

Palette

Newspaper

Full-size template

Gift tag template

1. Outline the design with black outliner. Let it dry completely, then paint in the body of the snowman with white paint, taking care not to paint over the outlines.

2. Protect the work surface with newspaper. While the white paint is still wet, sprinkle the head and body of the snowman with glitter. Leave your work to dry.

3. Brush off any loose glitter from the sections which have not yet been painted.

4. Paint the hat bobble white, then paint in all the red areas of the design.

141

5. Varying the colours to produce a pleasing effect, paint in the hatband and the scarf.

6. Fill in the background arch with diluted turquoise paint. Set your work aside to dry.

7. Cut out the snowman design and fix it to the holographic card with spray adhesive. Cut off the excess.

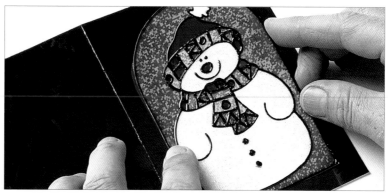

8. Score and fold the blue mirror card. Coat the back of the holographic card with spray adhesive and press it into place.

9. Add blobs of white outliner over the pale turquoise sky to represent snowflakes, and allow them to dry.

The finished card

*The pattern used for the scarf and hatband has
been repeated to produce a matching gift tag.*

Templates

Note

The card templates on this page have been reduced in size. To use, blow up on a photocopier at 150 percent.

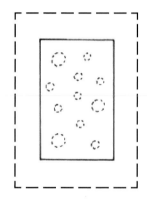

gift tags

Metal & Wire

by Julie Hickey

Two incredibly talented ladies who I met at craft shows, Vesta Abel and Jana Ewy, are totally responsible for my love of metal and wire. Vesta showed me that techniques from quilting to embossing could be applied to metal, and that stunning things happened when you heated it. Vesta's work really was art from her heart. Jana Ewy was using the copper with coloured foil sheets and adding wire accents to her outstanding work.

I have taken all that I have learned from these remarkable ladies and turned it into my own creative projects. I hope you will enjoy them and that they will inspire you to see what you can achieve with metal and wire.

Julie

Metal techniques

Rubbing

Found objects can be great to create rubbings from. It is easier with foil than with metal sheets. Place the foil over your found object, such as a shell, and use the wooden tool or embossing tool to rub and trace the patterns and markings on it.

Heating

You can only do this with pure copper. Using a craft heating tool, electric or gas hob or hot air gun paint stripper, heat the metal. It will change from bright copper to burnished orange to pink and then to purple. Finally it goes from blue to silvery gold.

Hammering

Create wonderful texture on the metal or foil by hammering. Use the large end of the embossing tool while resting on the foam sheet, and hammer the metal. Work so that the markings are close together.

Punching

Use different shaped metal cutters to cut out shapes in metal and foil.

Embossing

Use the embossing tool to create patterns on the metal or foil with a foam sheet beneath your work to help absorb the pattern.

Crimping

Feed the metal or foil through the rollers of the crimper to create a fabulous corrugated effect.

Wire techniques

Crimping

Feed the wire through the rollers on the crimper, and hey presto! Beautifully crimped wire. This works best with 22g or 26g wire.

Hammering

Once you have bent and shaped some wire, you can use a hammer and anvil to give your work a beaten look. This works best with 18g and 22g wire.

Winding and wrapping

I have used 26g wire to wrap around metal and foil. I found it easier to attach the end of the wire to the back of the piece with double-sided tape before beginning.

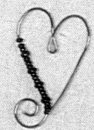

Beading

I used seed beads when wrapping my work, so I needed 26g wire. If you use bigger beads, you could change to 22g wire.

Sparkle

Add glitter glue to a piece of shaped and beaten wire to give extra sparkle and lift to your work.

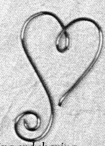

Bending and shaping

Round-nosed pliers are great to start the bending and shaping of the wire, then let your fingers take over. This works well with 18g, 22g and 26g wire.

Beaded Squares

Using just a few techniques, you can start your creative journey into metal and wire cards. In the following steps you will discover that heating a sheet of copper will give you many beautiful variations of random colour.

The techniques in this project include punching out squares, crimping wire, wrapping with wire and adding beads to give another dimension to your work.

You will need
Copper metal (1 sheet)

Black square card blank: 13cm^2 (5^1/$_8$in^2)

Cardboard 2.5cm (1in) squares

Red 26g wire (1 reel)

Seed and bugle beads

Scissors

Heating tool

Chopping board

Metal ruler

Craft knife

Square punch

Crimper

Double-sided tape

Wire cutters

Heating tool safety
Always heat metal on a heat-proof surface such as a chopping board. Remember that the metal conducts the heat, so if you are holding it with your fingers, keep them well away from the area you are heating. You can hold the metal with a wooden peg to be absolutely safe.

1. Put the copper on to a heat-proof surface such as a chopping board. Heat the copper with a heating tool, holding the tool 2.5cm (1in) away from the metal. Apply more heat in some areas than others in order to achieve a variety of colour effects, from burnished orange to purple to silvery blue.

2. Punch nine squares using a square hole punch.

3. Apply double-sided tape to the cardboard tiles. Peel off the backing and stick the tiles to the copper squares.

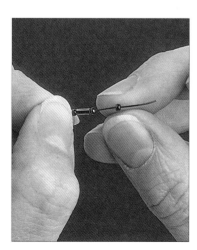

4. Thread beads on to a piece of uncrimped wire.

5. Put a piece of double-sided tape on the back of one of the copper-covered tiles and stick the end of the beaded wire to it.

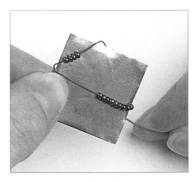

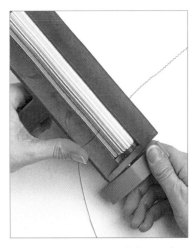

6. Wrap the beaded wire round the square so that the beads show at the front. Trim with wire cutters and secure at the back with another piece of double-sided tape.

7. Crimp a piece of the red wire using a crimper.

8. Wrap some of the copper tiles with beaded wire, some with crimped wire and some with plain wire. Leave some of them unwrapped. Mount the squares on your card using double-sided tape.

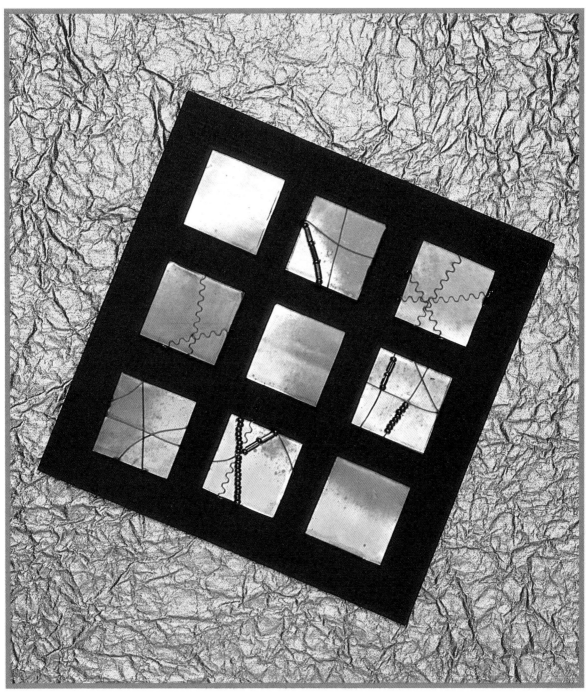

*The variation in the colours of the metal, set off by plain, crimped and beaded wire,
creates this stunning card.*

Put your new skills to work and create very different-looking cards, using the same techniques. Shaped, beaded wire creates beautiful plant forms in the butterfly card, whilst punched card sets off the heated copper square. Wrapped, heated copper hearts make a lovely card for Valentine's Day, a wedding or anniversary. Nine copper squares are stuck directly on to a shimmering gun-metal grey card, and set off with a beaded wire heart accent. Leaf shapes are great for wrapping with wire: this one is also mounted on open 6.3mm (¼in) mesh.

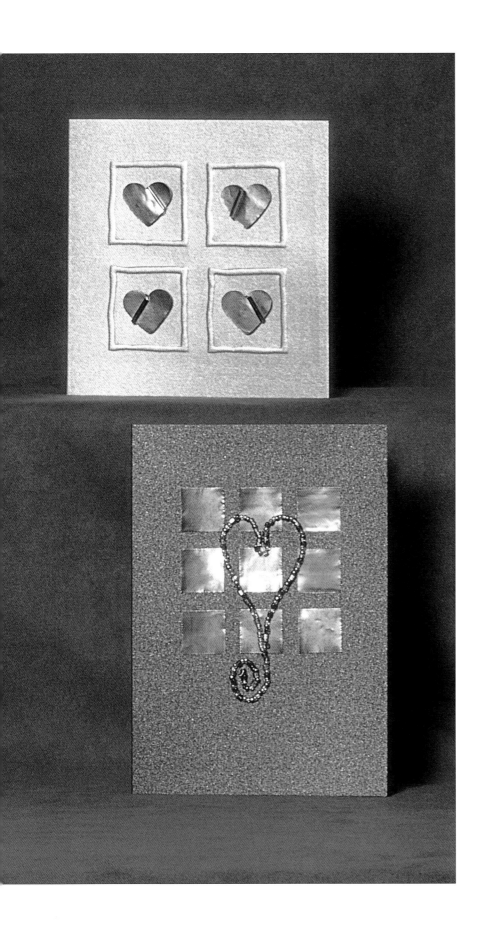

Polymer Clay

by Candida Woodhouse

I have always loved shapes and colours. Some of my earliest toys are still fresh in my memory; in particular, I can remember the feel of the wooden diamond pieces from a mosaic set, their bright colours and the satisfaction of slotting them neatly into place. If you are the sort of person who regularly arranges your coloured pencils into a rainbow inside their tin (so they look good enough to eat each time you open it), then you think like me!

This desire to play with shape and colour has never left me and it has found an outlet in numerous crafts over the years. Significantly, out of all the craft phases I have gone through: knitting, painting, scale model aircraft, jigsaw puzzles and modelling with anything from paper straws to matchsticks, polymer clay has lasted the longest. This may have something to do with the fact that, with polymer clay, you are master of both shape and colour. It has to be the most versatile craft medium I have ever used, as well as one of the simplest.

My first dabblings with clay came about while I was living in the British Virgin Islands. Although the lifestyle there is simple and uncomplicated, I could never go long without wanting to create something with my hands, and working with clay satisfied this urge. What caught my imagination and sparked my interest was an example of a *millefiori* cane in a children's craft book. I was fascinated by the potential of such a technique, not least because I always loved finding out how things worked – and this is the way the traditional English confectionery rock is formed!

I launched straight into cane work and used the results to cover foil armatures in the shape of dolphins, shells and starfish which made ideal Christmas tree decorations. The Caribbean also had to be the perfect place to go crazy with loud colours! The vibrancy of nature's colours in the tropics is unique; the sea an unimaginable array of azure blues, teal and ultramarine, whilst the flowers are saturated with intense hues of every shade. These bright colours are reflected in the card designs that you will find in the following pages.

It may be clay, but you do not have to be a skilled sculptor to produce some fantastic results. Greetings cards are a great beginning, providing as they do a miniature canvas on which to work. I hope that the simplicity of my designs are apparent and that they will convince even the most timid craftsperson to give it a go.

Candida

Lovable Bear

The body parts of the little bear on this card are all hand modelled by hand, then the details are added with a modelling tool. A small cutter is used to make the heart that he is happily hugging to his chest. The base card is a ready-made card blank decorated with red foil.

When you have made this version of him, think about other activities he can get up to! He could, for instance, hold a bunch of flowers for a *Get Well Soon* card, sit next to another bear for a *Best Friends* card, or he could gaze up at a moon as a *Thinking of You* card.

You will need

Brown, red and black clay

Heart-shaped cutter

Craft knife

Small- and medium-size ball-ended modelling tools

Clay shaper

Two-fold, white card with heart-shaped aperture, folded to 9 x 10.5cm (3½ x 4¼in)

7.5cm (3in) square of red foil paper

Self-adhesive sticky pads

Fast-acting paper glue

Instant glue

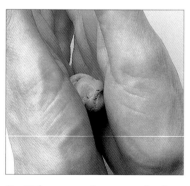

1. Use a blunt craft knife to cut some clay from the block. Store the rest of the clay in resealable plastic bags to keep it from drying out.

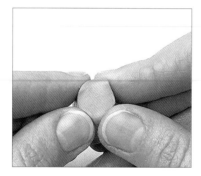

2. Start softening the clay by squeezing it between your fingers and thumbs.

3. When you have worked the piece of clay into a rough ball, roll it smooth between the palms of your hands.

4. When all signs of cracking have disappeared, roll the clay into a log shape.

5. Use the blunt craft knife to cut the log into three pieces – one for the body, one for the head and one for the arms, legs, ears and feet.

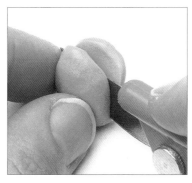

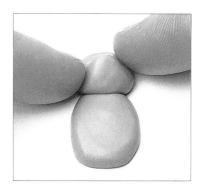

6. Roll the body piece into an oval, flatten it with your finger then smooth the edges to form the body.

7. If you make the body shape too fat, cut a thin slice of clay off the back.

8. Work the head shape then press on to the body.

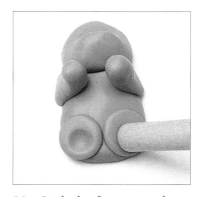

9. Roll a small log for the arms. Cut this in half, then stick the cut end of each arm on to the body, leaving arms sticking straight up.

10. Roll two small balls for the feet, then flatten them with your finger.

11. Stick the feet on to the body, then use the medium-size ball-end modelling tool to impress the paw pads.

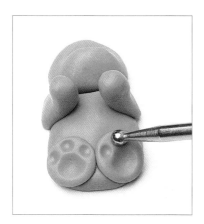

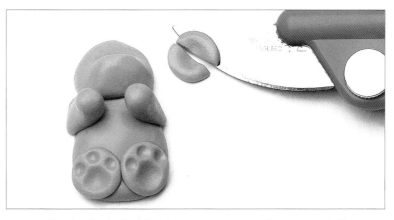

12. Use the small ball-end modelling tool to impress the toe pads.

13. Roll a ball of clay for the ears, press it flat, use a ball-ended modelling tool to impress the centre, then cut it in half. Use the craft knife to lift each ear off the tile.

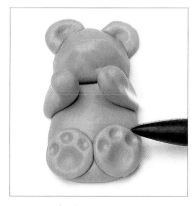

14. Stick the ears to the head, then use the clay shaper to neaten all the body parts, smoothing the joins between the parts to ensure they are secure.

15. Use the small ball-ended tool to impress the eye sockets. Roll two tiny black balls for the eyes, then gently press them into the sockets.

16. Roll a small oval of black clay for the nose, then stick this on to the head.

17. Flatten a small piece of red clay to form a 2mm ($^1/_{16}$in) thick disc, then use the cutter to make the heart.

18. Carefully lift away the excess clay with a craft knife, then, still using the knife, lift the heart so that it is not marked by your fingers.

19. Soften the edges of the heart, place it in position, then fold the arms down to hold the heart. Bake the finished model in an oven.

20. Position four sticky pads round the heart-shaped cut out.

21. Stick the square of red foil face down on the sticky pads.

22. Apply paper glue to the back of centre section of the card, then fold the left-hand flap down to secure.

23. Apply two blobs of instant glue to the back of the bear, then set him down in the centre of the red heart.

The finished card together with a matching gift tag

Elephant

This little elephant is literally overflowing with sentiment, he has too much love to contain! He is also easier to make than you might think. Look carefully, and you will see that his body and head are just two overlapping circles, his ears are two large teardrop shapes, his feet are parts of circles, and his trunk is a moulded log of clay. Using two or three different sized cutters for the heart shapes gives more depth to the overall design.

Heart Pendant

The pendant is a card and a gift all in one! The modelled heart is trimmed with white clay and ruffled using a blunt pointed tool. A jewellery eye pin was inserted before baking. I varnished the heart when it was cold and mounted it on a sumptuous velour paper with a lace-trimmed aperture. The gold chain is taped temporarily to the inside of the card for presentation.

Wedding Cake

This project introduces two new techniques – colour blending and cane work. I find it very satisfying to see a new colour gradually appear from two others and, if you want a lovely marbled effect, you could stop anywhere along the way. Here I make three shades of pink using white and deep pink clays.

The three pinks are rolled into flat sheets, cut into thin strips, then built up into a multicoloured log (cane). The cane is then rolled down to a smaller diameter and sliced to form the roses that adorn the wedding cake. Do not be nervous of making the cane as this is a very forgiving one for a first attempt. Hopefully you will be inspired to try others!

You will need

White, dark pink and green clay

Craft knife

Clay shaper

Single-fold, mauve card, 10cm (4in) square

Piece of white card, 9cm (3½in) square

Piece of purple foil paper, 6cm (2½in) square

Fancy-edged scissors

Paper glue

Instant glue

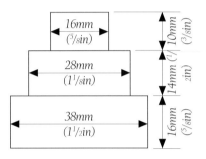

Full-size pattern for the three-tier cake

1. Using the same amounts of white clay with small amounts of dark pink clay, make three different shades of pink by rolling them together between your palms.

2. As the log lengthens, fold it in half. Repeat the rolling and folding until the colours merge into one shade.

3. Roll the three shades of pink clay into flat sheets, then use a craft knife to cut each sheet into narrow strips, varying the width randomly between 3 and 6mm ($^1/_8$ and $^1/_4$in).

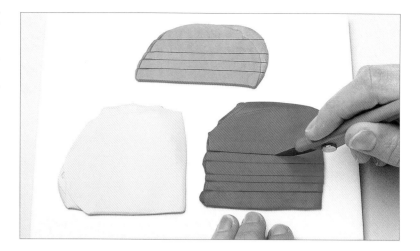

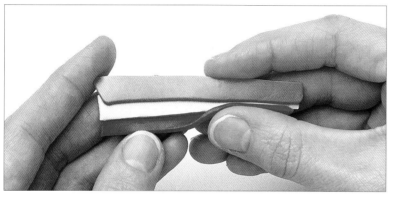

4. Assemble the coloured strip into one multicoloured log, overlapping contrasting shades as you build it up.

5. Continue building up the log, overlapping the joins until you have used up all the strips.

6. Compress the log firmly with your fingers to squeeze out any air bubbles, then roll it to reduce its diameter. When the log gets too long for the tile, cut in half and continue rolling until it is an appropriate size. For this project you need three different sized rolls – make the largest approximately 6mm ($^1/_4$in) in diameter and the smallest 4mm (just over $^1/_8$in)

7. If the clay becomes soft through handling, leave it to cool down, then use a sharp blade to cut each log into 2mm ($^1/_{16}$in) thick slices to create the roses.

8. Roll a 3mm ($^1/_8$in) thick sheet of white clay then cut out the three layers of the cake. Assemble the layers next to each other, then cut the corners with a craft knife. Smooth all edges with the clay shaper.

9. Roll a 3mm ($^1/_8$in) diameter log from the green clay and cut this into slices for the leaf shapes.

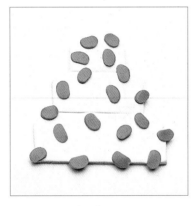

10. Press the leaves randomly along the joins of the cake.

11. Now add the roses, overlapping them on the leaves. Place the large roses at the bottom of the cake and the small ones at the top. Use the clay shaper to nudge each rose into position. When you are happy with the arrangement, bake the completed cake!

12. Draw a 9 x 9cm (3½ x 3½in) square on white card and cut round it with fancy-edged scissors. Then glue the white card and the purple foil panel on the front of the card. Finally glue the cake on to the card.

The finished card and a matching gift tag

Rubber Stamping

by Melanie Hendrick

I believe that within all of us there is creative potential waiting to be discovered or rediscovered and nurtured.

Some of my favourite creative memories are of making cards – for family, friends, overseas relatives on their birthdays, or to say 'thank you' or 'I miss you'. A greetings card can say so much, but a handmade card can say so much more.

I discovered the wonder of rubber stamping one cold and windy Saturday afternoon. A few days before, I had started a new job, and had been handed a pack of blank cards, a rubber stamp and a multi-coloured inkpad. 'Go home and make some cards', I was instructed. Making cards was fine, no problem, but what was I supposed to do with this wooden block with a rubber image adhered to it? Over the years, I had printed from potatoes (when I was six) and from hand-carved lino, but I had never heard of rubber stamping before. To me, stamping was something the Post Office did!

With some curiosity, I picked up the stamp and inked it with the multi-coloured inkpad, and stamped a sunflower on to a piece of card. Wow! Like a woman possessed, I stamped every piece of card I had, plus envelopes, and even the pages of my diary – anything I could get my hands on. I was hooked.

Four years on, my enthusiasm hasn't waned. As you try the projects that follow, you will discover that rubber stamping opens up a whole new creative world. The humble blank card has been replaced with wonderful textures, vibrant colour and even decorated matchboxes! Nothing is unstampable when you have a little know-how.

I have heard rubber stamping described as good therapy and highly addictive, and I agree – what a wonderful and healthy way to spend your time! So put aside any fears or household chores, order takeaway for the family and join me on a creative adventure full of discovery and lots of fun.

Happy stamping!

Basic techniques

The basic stamping technique shown below applies whether you are stamping with embossing ink, for use with embossing powder, or with coloured inks or paints. Follow these procedures, and you will not end up with smudged, uneven or multiple stamped images.

The facing page shows how to apply embossing powder to an image stamped with embossing ink. When you heat the embossing powder, the image becomes raised and shiny.

There is a rainbow of embossing powder colours available, and you can buy scented, metallic, pearlescent, glitter, fine detail or thick heavy duty powders.

Tinted embossing inkpads are useful, because they allow you to see where you have stamped before you apply the embossing powder. Clear embossing inkpads are good for art embossing with heavy duty powders.

You will need
Rubber stamp
Heating tool
Anti-static bag
Tinted embossing inkpad
Embossing powder
Card
Scissors

1. Wipe the anti-static bag over the card. This means that the powder will only bind to the inked, stamped area, and will not spill over the rest of the card.

2. Take the inkpad to the stamp and ink the stamp with a light tapping motion. Do not wipe the pad over the stamp, as this will produce an uneven stamp.

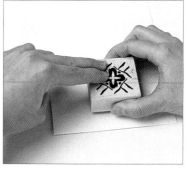

3. Position the stamp on the card using the hand you write with. Take your other hand and press lightly over the whole area with two fingers. Do not rock the stamp, or you will get multiple images.

4. Hold the card down with your second hand and lift the stamp off cleanly with your first hand. This tinted embossing inkpad leaves only a very faint image, which will act as a base for the embossing powder.

Tip
Remember to replace the inkpad lid when you have finished, to prevent embossing powder from damaging your inkpad.

5. Sprinkle embossing powder on to the stamped area. To avoid waste, it is best to transfer a little powder to a small tub.

6. Pour the excess powder back into the tub.

7. Use a heating tool to heat the powder – a hairdryer will blow it away. Hold the heating tool 4cm (1½in) away from the design and work from one corner across the design, in one motion. Do not use a to-and-fro hair-drying action, as this will heat unevenly.

When I first tried rubber stamping using embossing powder, and saw it go from matte and flat to glossy and raised, outlining my stamped image, I jumped up and down with excitement. It looked so professional and the possibilities seemed endless. Here are some of the effects you can create using the embossed image shown above.

171

Purple Pyramid

Stamping on to textured surfaces and metal can be great fun. The results are not always predictable, but that is part of the creative adventure.

I am known for my hoarding and recycling habits. I keep all my scraps, elements and stamping mishaps in themed trays. I theme in colours: for example, in my earthy trays I have scraps of metal and handpainted backgrounds in terracotta and verdigris.

This system is ideal when you want to create a collage, as with this card. I have taken all my scraps of handmade paper in a particular range of colours, torn them up and pasted them on to a black background. Collage is one of the most instinctive and creative of all techniques. Even under the studio lights, I found myself starting to hum with enjoyment as I created this one. Just relax into it, paste on one strip at a time and see what emerges.

You will need
Stamps
Handmade paper
A5 white card
Gold paint
Coloured ink
Gold pigment ink
A5 size black card blank
Split pin
Wire • Mesh • Metal
Round-nosed pliers
Double-sided tape
Matte acrylic glue
Wide, flat-headed 1in brush
Pastry brushes
Coloured and metallic pearlised pigments
Gold glitter spray
Gold heavy duty embossing powder
Heat tool • 3D fluid
Single hole punch

1. Take a piece of A5 white card. Apply a matte acrylic glue with a wide, flat-headed 1in brush. Tear pieces of handmade or hand-painted paper and stick them down, black first, darker to lighter. Lay down torn bits of paper and coat them with glue.

Tip
If you struggle with colour matching, why not put together a colour scrapbook? Fill it with fashion, home décor images from magazines or colour swatches that inspire you. I also keep samples from collages of mine that have really worked, for future inspiration.

2. While the collage is still wet, dip a pastry brush or chunky paintbrush into pearlised pigments and shake the powder over the collage. Use a different brush for each colour, and shake on the metallic pigments last. Pat the powder in to the wet glue with the brushes.

3. While the collage is still wet, ink an abstract pattern stamp with a colour and stamp randomly over the collage.

4. Before the coloured stamping is dry, stamp with a complementary stamp using gold paint. Set aside to dry.

5. Spray gold glitter spray over the collage, holding the spray 30cm (11¾in) away and spraying a light mist. This helps to seal your collage. Then leave to dry.

6. Ink up the abstract pattern stamp with coloured ink and set it aside.

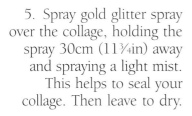

7. On a 1.5 x 4cm (½ x 1½in) piece of metal, stamp the swirl design randomly in gold pigment ink. Sprinkle it with gold heavy duty embossing powder.

8. Heat and while still warm, stamp using the complementary pre-inked stamp. Set aside to cool.

9. Take an A5 size black card blank and cut out a triangle with a 13cm (5in) base. At 6.5cm (2½in) across, measure 19cm (7½in) up to the point.

10. Apply double-sided tape round the edges of one black triangle. Peel off the backing. Position collaged paper over the triangle. Use the triangle as a template and trim round it. Keep excess collaged pieces to use later.

11. Take a 3.5 x 8cm (1³⁄₈ x 2¼in) piece of card. Put double-sided tape round the edges. Stick a spare collaged piece to it and cut round, using the card as a template.

12. Glue the embossed metal to the collage-decorated piece of card. Apply 3D fluid on to the collaged card round the edge of the metal but not over it. Set it aside to dry clear overnight.

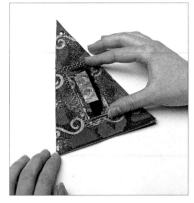

13. Punch a hole in the top of both triangles and attach them with a split pin. Glue the mesh to the pyramid card. Glue the metal and collage strip to the mesh.

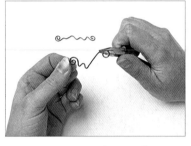

14. Using round-nosed pliers, bend a piece of coloured wire into shape. Clip the pliers on the end of the wire and bend it round to make a spiral. Do the same at the other end. Then clip on to the wire at different points along its length and bend it to make kinks.

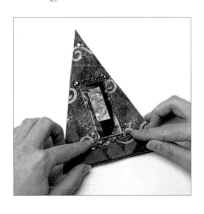

15. Glue the shaped wire on to the mesh.

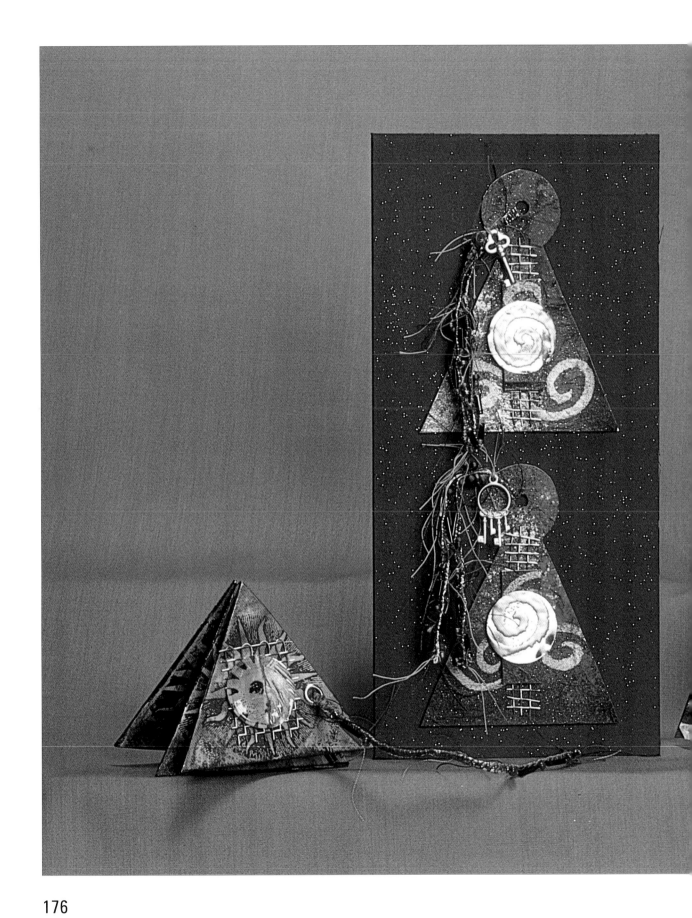

Carry on the pyramid theme, adding charms and tassels to further enhance the luxurious quality of your cards. The small pyramids open out like a concertina so that you can write your message inside. The tall black card features faux door locks and key charms used with fold, purple and turquoise. Note that black and white can look just as effective as bright colours. In the tall pyramid card, bold spiral designs, contrasting textures and silver metal and mesh are used to spectacular effect.

Embossing

by Carol Wallis

I started crafting several years ago but, after dabbling in many different crafts, I found myself looking for something new. Luckily, I was visiting my local craft store when a very brief demonstration of stencil embossing was given. Short though it was – only over a lunch break – it was enough for me to be hooked! I bought some brass stencils and an embossing tool, and began a passion that has been with me ever since.

At first I had no books, instructions or tutor so I taught myself. Though I made lots of mistakes, somehow good things always emerged from them, so it was a relatively painless process. Almost before I knew it, I was producing professional cards that were inspiring others to want to learn stencil embossing, which is also known as dry embossing.

I have not looked back since the owner of my local craft store asked *me* to give an in-store demonstration. From little acorns, as the saying goes, and before long I began to teach and demonstrate regularly. I have made live television appearances and written articles for magazines, and I also demonstrate regularly at craft shows. I love the challenge of thinking up different ways to use stencils, and I really enjoy meeting all the people who are curious enough to come and see what I do.

One of the best things about this craft is that anyone can do it. My youngest student so far was five, and the oldest eighty-four! Both of them produced fantastic cards in next to no time. It gives me a real thrill when other people discover how simple it is to create beautiful cards, and to see their pride in what they have achieved.

I hope you enjoy making these projects as much as I did, and that they will inspire you to create lots of beautiful cards.

Daisy, Daisy

This is a good design to start with as it uses only one sheet of card and one stencil. The stencil is moved around so that its different elements form a pleasing composition. Colour is added using chalk, starting with the lightest and building up to the darkest. Use a chalk eraser to remove any stray marks before assembling the finished card. To give a professional-looking finish and a raised effect, the completed design is mounted on layers of card, each of which is edged with a different colour.

If you are worried about mounting the layers evenly, a good tip is to place the top left corner of each card first, which makes it easier to line up. This is because, if you read from left to right, your eye is automatically drawn to that area.

You will need

Daisy stencil: Lasting
Impressions L528

White card about 19 x 15cm
(7½ x 6in) for mount

White card, two pieces each
about 15 x 8cm (6 x 3¾in)

Low-tack adhesive tape

Wax paper sheet

Light box

Embossing tool with large
ball tip

Sponge-tipped applicators

Chalk: light, medium and
deep yellow; orange; light and
medium green

Craft knife or scalpel and
cutting mat, and / or small
craft guillotine

Cotton ball

Adhesive putty

Double-sided tape

Chalk eraser

The chalks

The stencil I used

1. Fix the stencil to the card with low-tack adhesive tape.

180

2. Flip the card and place it on the light box. Apply wax to the back of the design.

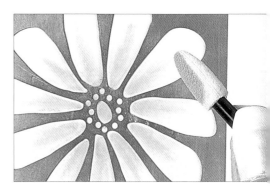

3. Using the large ball of the embossing tool, work round the long sides and the top of the stencil. Emboss the flower and swirl, but not the leaf.

4. Remove from the light box and flip, leaving the stencil in place. Stroke pale yellow chalk on the flower centre and part-way down the petals.

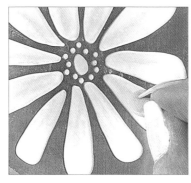

5. Add mid-yellow chalk, but do not take it so far down each petal. Work from the base of the petal towards the tip.

6. Add deep yellow chalk, using just a little towards the centre of each petal.

7. Holding the applicator upright, dab orange chalk in the flower centre and stroke a faint line down each petal.

8. Colour the swirl in blended greens. Remove the stencil.

9. Reposition the stencil so the leaf is at the bottom of the card.

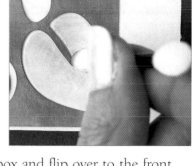

10. Flip your work and place on the light box. Apply wax over the leaf and emboss it.

11. Take the card off the light box and flip over to the front. Start to fill in the leaf with light green. Add dark green from the centre outwards but not right to the edge.

12. Reposition the stencil so the second swirl mirrors the first. Place on the light box, wax and emboss. Remove from the light box and colour in the second swirl.

13. Replace the stencil in its original position. Working on the light box, wax and emboss the remaining outline at the lower edge of the card, but do not go over the leaf shape.

14. Use adhesive putty to remove any tape residue from your work.

15. Replace the stencil and, using a cotton ball, rub on a blend of yellow chalks to colour the edge. Do not tape the stencil down for this stage.

16. Edge the second small piece of card with greenchalk, then fold the mount card in half and colour the front edges with deep yellow chalk.

17. Trim 6mm (¼in) from the edge of the project card using a craft knife or guillotine. Trim 3mm (⅛in) from the card with the green edge.

18. Layer the cards on the card mount to check the effect. Fix the cards in place, a layer at a time, using double-sided tape.

Tip
You can buy double-sided tape in a small dispenser, which is a useful and economical way to attach designs to a card mount.

The finished card

Card and matching envelope

The matching envelope was produced very simply by colouring the edges of a plain white envelope with yellow chalk, then laying on the stencil and chalking in the leaves. When you do this, use a spare piece of card to prevent the flap being marked by the chalk.

It is really easy to change the look of this card by using different colours of chalk for the design, or by using metallic or pearlised card. Remove any stray chalk marks or dust afterwards using a chalk eraser. There is no need to fix the chalk.

These examples show how you can move the stencils around to create different designs, and how changing the colours of the chalk can give a completely different effect. The purple daisy card (below left and cover) has been given a 3D effect using the techniques covered in the Tiny Toes project (see page 186), with a simple torn paper base. The delicate blue card in the centre was produced on vellum.

Tiny Toes

This versatile card would be perfect as a birthday card for a little girl, or to welcome a new arrival. The variations on page 190–191 show a version made with a different stencil which is more suitable to give to a little boy.

To make the frame for the card, emboss round the straight edges of the stencil first, then emboss the details of the shoes. Take care to leave enough space between the stencil and the edge of the card before embossing. When you cut out the shoe shapes you need to leave a good margin or you will lose the embossed effect.

The card is assembled using pieces of foam tape, which hold them slightly apart and produce a 3D effect. There is a lot of detail and it may look fiddly, but you will find tweezers very helpful during the assembly process. You do not have to use as many layers of card as I have done, but I think it makes the finished card look extra-special. Complete the effect with an envelope decorated to match and trimmed with tiny rosebuds (see pages 188–189).

You will need

Shoe stencil: Lasting Impressions L9130

White card for mount 21 x 13cm (8¼ x 5¼in)

Pale green card 13 x 10cm (5¼ x 4in)

Dotted pink card 12 x 9cm (4¾ x 3½ in)

Deep pink card: will be trimmed to 10.5 x 7.5cm (4¼ x 3in)

Scraps of card in pale and deep pink, pink dotted and green

Light box

Low-tack adhesive tape

Wax paper sheet

Embossing tool with large ball tip

Fancy craft scissors

Straight scissors

Craft knife and cutting mat

Tacky craft adhesive

Tweezers

Hole punch

Double-sided tape and 3D foam pads

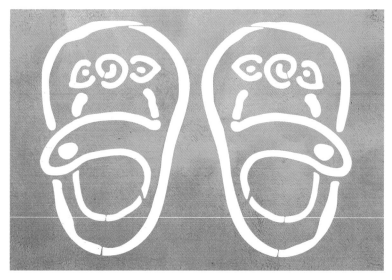

The stencil

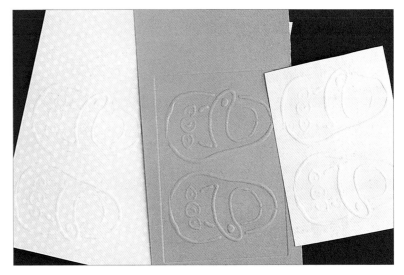

1. Fix the stencil to the deep pink card with low-tack tape and place on the light box. Wax the card and emboss shoe shapes and a frame. Emboss shoe shapes on pink dotted and pale pink card.

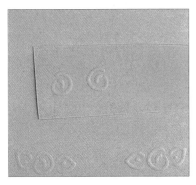

2. Emboss two roses on a scrap of deep pink card, and roses and leaves on a scrap of pale green card.

3. Cut outside the embossed frame of the deep pink card using fancy craft scissors.

4. Cut out the pink dotted shoe shapes carefully on the *inside* of the embossed line.

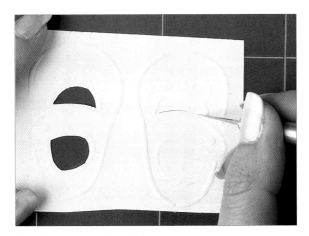

5. Place the pale pink card on a cutting mat and use a craft knife or scalpel to cut out the sections of shoe above and below the embossed straps.

6. Using scissors, cut carefully round the shoe shapes on the outside of the line, leaving a border of at least 1mm (^{1}/$_{16}$in) round the embossed line.

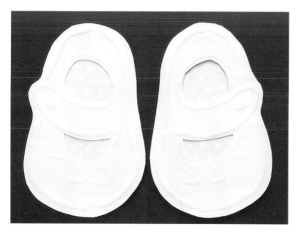

7. Place the pale pink shoe 'uppers' on the dotted 'insoles' and fix them together using tacky craft adhesive.

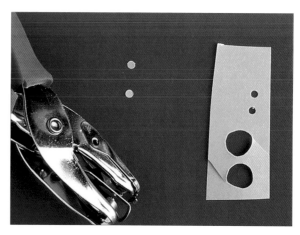

8. Using a craft knife and cutting mat, cut out the two pink rosebuds. Using a hole punch, make two tiny circles from the same card.

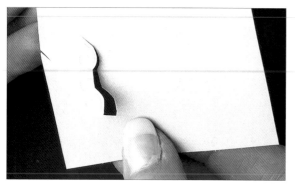

9. Using scissors, cut round the leaves and across between them to form a 'bridge' on which to place the pink rosebud.

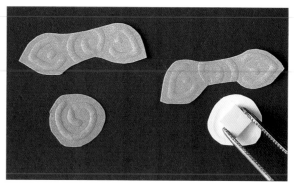

10. Using tweezers, place tiny double-sided adhesive foam pads on the back of each rosebud, then fix to the leaves.

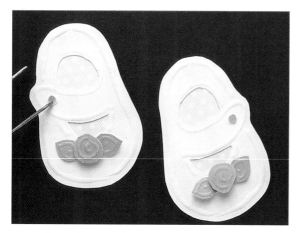

11. Place the rosebuds and leaves on the front of the shoes and the 'buttons' on the straps. Fix in place with tacky craft adhesive.

Tip
To place the buttons, apply adhesive to the strap first. Moisten the end of the tweezers as it will help to pick up the dots more easily.

Make a matching envelope by gluing an embossed panel of card to the front of a plain envelope. Decorate with tiny buds and leaves.

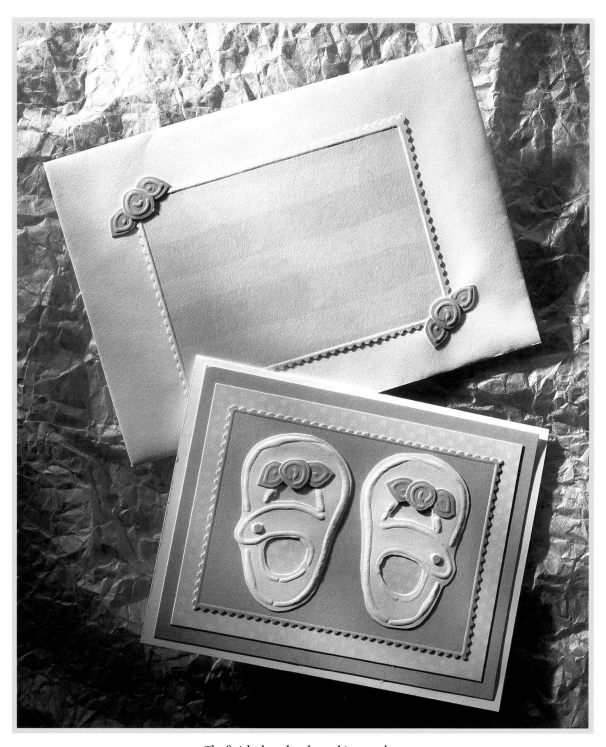

The finished card and matching envelope

*The card was completed by layering the backing cards and
fixing the shoes in place using double-sided tape.*

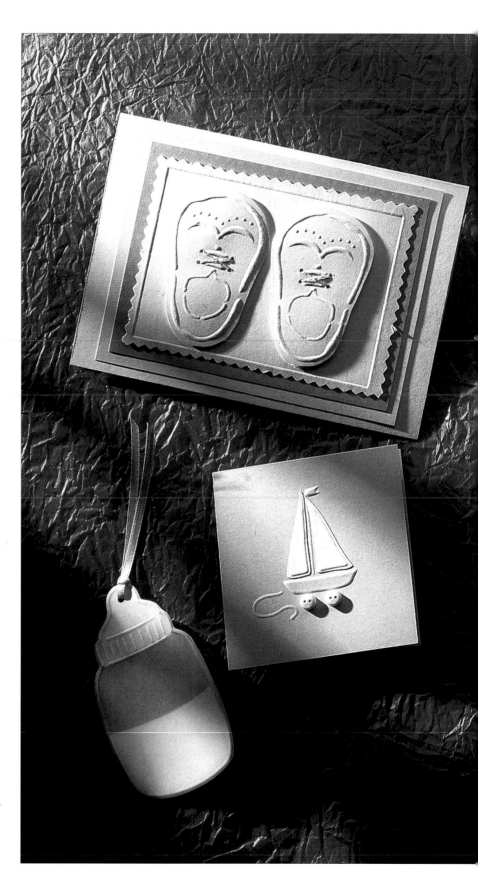

These cards were made using a variety of stencils on a nursery theme. The card featuring shoes for a boy was finished with silver thread laces. The baby's bottle gift tag (below left) was cut from vellum and outlined, then a piece of white card was placed behind the vellum to produce a convincing 'milk' effect. The top was added using embossed pastel card with a ribbon trim. The little yacht (centre left) was finished with two tiny button 'wheels' and an embossed string, and the buttons on the tiny sleepsuit (top right) were made using a hole punch. The clothes and toy on the line of 'washing' (below right) were made using scraps of card in different pastel colours, and the 'pegs' and washing line were coloured using chalk.

Index